DUET

Conversational Chin

for Beginners

(formerly titled: Chinese in Your Pocket)

by MORRIS SWADESH

Dover Publications, Inc., New York

Published in Canada by General Publishing Company, Ltd., 30 Lesmill Road, Don Mills, Toronto, Ontario.
Published in the United Kingdom by Constable and Company, Ltd., 10 Orange Street, London W. C. 2.

This Dover edition, first published in 1964, is an unabridged republication of the work first published by Henry Holt and Company in 1948 under the former title: *Chinese in Your Pocket.*

Standard Book Number: 486-21123-1

Library of Congress Catalog Card Number: 64-15506

Manufactured in the United States of America
Dover Publications, Inc.
180 Varick Street
New York, N. Y. 10014

To the
CHINESE PEOPLE

whose characteristic friendliness and patience make learning their language a pleasure.

With special appreciation to my Chinese and American co-workers who helped develop and test out in practical teaching this plan for putting Chinese into your pocket and onto your tongue: Raymond Hsu, Shih-Hui Hua, Shih-Yi Li, J. E. McDonald, Julian Steuer, Lui-Ho Tung, Chuen-Shang Wang, To-An Wang, Chen-Ning Yang.

And with sincere gratitude to Prof. Yuen Ren Chao for his careful examination of the ms. and his help toward making the English and the Chinese match in spirit as well as in sense.

M. S.

FOREWORD

THERE ARE many pocket-size introductions to Chinese, but few which do so much in so little space as *Chinese in Your Pocket*. Dr. Swadesh's experience in organizing rapid courses for various languages right on the field in Burma and in China has resulted in a book of a live language with live material for use in live situations. But don't take this for one of those handbooks made up in a hurry for men of supposedly low I. Q. to get a smattering of pidgin Chinese. While the style of exposition may be deceptively informal and colloquial, the stuff behind it is basically the same as what you would learn—or ought to—as part of a more formal academic course.

There is no need to enumerate all the special features of the book, which will speak for themselves. But I should like to mention especially the following:

(1) The "learning tips" give the essence of language learning without the paraphernalia of linguistic terminology —which both the author and I love so much.

(2) The system of romanization used here is in general agreement with recent trends. You can't forget to *un*aspirate your *p*'s and *t*'s if they are written as *b*'s and *d*'s to start with.

(3) The over-all characteristic of informality in both the style of description and the language taught not only makes the subject matter interesting, but also brings home the truth that this is the language of real people in their everyday talk.

(4) After you have learned the main structure of the language thru the varied forms of model sentences, the appended Practical Dictionary will enable you to fill in the gaps of your knowledge with practical ideas for saying something new each time.

It is not expected that mastering the contents of this book will give you many hours of college credit or make you talk like a Chinese, in vocabulary, idiom, and style. That must come with prolonged and painstaking study. But seeing that so much of the learning of Chinese has had to consist of the unlearning of wrong things, I am sure that with *Chinese in Your Pocket* in your pocket you will be that much farther ahead.

YUEN REN CHAO

Cambridge, Massachusetts

PLAN OF ATTACK

SUMMARY OF LEARNING TIPS

1. Imitate: Learn to speak understandably by imitating people.

2. Read, speak, listen: When you *see* the Chinese words, *say* them out loud, so you can *hear* them.

3. Use your head: Figure out ways of getting your meaning across.

4. Use Chinese models: Don't translate word for word from English.

5. Use a few memory aids: Find English words that remind you of the Chinese.

6. Speak up: Talk every chance you get.

7. Repeat new words: When you hear a new word, say it out loud.

8. Keep smiling: Be friendly so that people will talk to you.

9. Ask two-way questions: Is it a this or a that?

EXPLANATIONS

A Method for Talking Soon

OF COURSE, *Chinese in Your Pocket* isn't intended to stay in your pocket. It is arranged so you can very soon be sliding its words off your tongue, talking Chinese fairly easily and very understandably. You can be doing this after fifteen to thirty hours spent in learning the following few tricks:

1. You must be able to get the sound of the words from the spelled form (First Session). Later on (especially in the Fifth and Ninth Sessions), you can improve your pronunciation by listening to and imitating the native Chinese with the help of the suggestions and exercises given in this book. Many people have acquired a real native flavor to their Chinese in just this way.

2. You must master about 50 simple basic sentences (Sessions 2, 6, 10, 13), get to know them so well that they are always on the tip of your tongue.

3. You must get the knack of using the basic sentences in practical situations (Practical Exercises), combining them with each other and with gestures, so that they will get all sorts of meanings across.

4. You must learn to take a word out of the Practical Dictionary and fit it into one of the basic sentences in a way that makes good understandable Chinese.

5. You must have fluent knowledge of a few sentences in Chinese for asking people to speak slowly and clearly, and you must know how to ask questions that have to be an-

swered simply with words you can understand. (See especially Tip 9 on Two-Way Questions, p. 30).

The first part of this book is for learning the tricks we have mentioned. The second part is a Practical Dictionary, which gives the simplest Chinese corresponding to common words in English. The aim is to have a dictionary that is small and easy to use; and also to get you to use the common words of Chinese over and over again in different situations, so that you will eventually get to know them and not have to look them up any more.

The language presented in this book is the official national tongue of China, known as the National Language or North Chinese or Mandarin. It is spoken, altho with many small variations, by over 400 million people in Northern, Central, and Western China. Of the other languages in China, some, like Cantonese, are related to Mandarin in the way that Swedish is related to English; and some, like Tibetan and Mongolian, are altogether different. Nevertheless, almost anywhere you go in China, you are likely to find a certain number of people who have learned the National Language, either in school or by travel in different parts of the country. Obviously, this is the best language for the visitor in China to learn. If you plan to settle in a non-Mandarin area, you will want to know the local language in addition.

The variations of Mandarin itself are apt to bother the new-comer in China, just as foreigners are confused by the differences in English as between Boston and Chicago, or as between London and Edinburgh. However, if you talk in the manner explained in this book, you will be quite easily understood by all who speak Mandarin. The chief difficulty comes when you try to understand them. For instance, you have to get used to the fact that much of central and western

China pronounces **san** for **shan** (mountain), and that some areas pronounce **yən** for **rən** (person) or **byən** for **bing** (soldier).

About the Spelling

The spelling of Chinese in this book is based on Dr. Yuen Ren Chao's Chinese National Romanization. The advantages of this choice are:

a. It gives an automatic pronunciation of the consonant sounds. That is, if you read the consonant letters with their usual English values, you make either a sound that is exactly right or something that is near enough so that people will have no trouble understanding you.

b. The representation of the vowel sounds is practically identical with that used in familiar spellings of Chinese place-names, such as Shanghai, Shansi, Hunan, etc. This means that anything you may happen to know or find out about the pronunciation of Chinese geographic names will help you learn to read all the other Chinese words in this book.

In a few small points, we depart from the rules of the National Romanization. These modifications are used only to make things still easier for the beginner:

a. The tones are shown by small arrows instead of by changes in the spelling of the syllable.

b. **Dj** is used instead of **j** to avoid confusion with the sound shown with this letter in other systems.

c. **Dz** is used in place of *tz*.

d. An **ə** (inverted *e*) is used for the slightly varying, but essentially single, sound shown by both *e* and *o*.

e. The combination **ir** is used instead of *y* for the special sound occurring after *s* and *sh* and other similar consonants.

f. The spelling **ung** is used in place of *ong*.

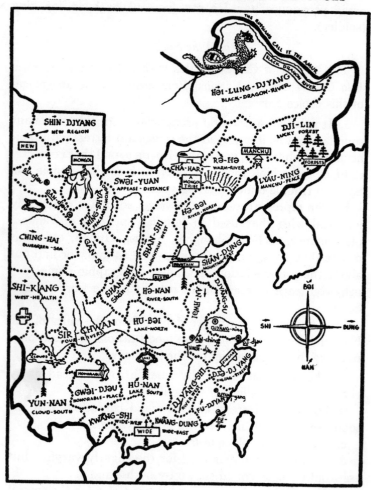

Explanations of these names will be found in the discussion on pages 1 to 7.

ON THE SOUNDS, BEGINNING

PLACE-NAMES AND PRONUNCIATION

Everyone is familiar with a certain number of Chinese place-names: cities, provinces, rivers, etc. You may possibly mispronounce some of them, either because of certain illogical things about the way the consonant letters are used in the conventional spellings, or because of not happening to know how the vowel letters are to be read. Nevertheless, the fact that you are familiar with these names makes it helpful to begin with them in learning to read romanized Chinese.

The Common Spellings

Be prepared for a few striking differences between the National Romanization and the conventional spellings. Here are some cases:

Spellings	*Romanization*	*Meanings*
Kirin	**Dji-lin**	Lucky-forest
Nanking	**Nan-djing**	South-capital
Kiangsi	**Djyang-shi**	River-west
Jehol	**Rə-hə**	Warm-river
Peiping	**Bəi-ping**	North-peace
Tientsin	**Tyan-djin**	Heaven-ferry
Kweichow	**Gwəi-djəu**	Honored-region

1

But a majority of the words appear the same in National Romanization as in the conventional spelling; thus: **Ching-hai** (Bluegreen-sea), **Hu-nan** (Lake-south), **Shan-dung** (Mountain-east).

Meanings as a Memory Help

In this lesson, you will also get considerable information about the meanings of Chinese place-names. This will make it easier for you to learn and remember the names. Furthermore, many of them tell something about where the place is; for example, **Hə-nan** (common spelling *Honan*) and **Hə-bəi** (common spelling *Hopei*) mean respectively *River-south* and *River-north* and are located south and north of the Yellow River. Study the map of the Chinese provinces on page xviii, and you will find you can remember most of the provinces after going over them once.

It is interesting to note that Chinese place-names often refer to desirable qualities and conditions, as **Dji-lin** (Lucky-forest), **Gwəi-djəu** (Honored-region), **Shi-kang** (West-health). The idea of *peace* is most frequent, as in **Bəi-ping** (North-peace), **An-djing** (Peace-felicitation), **Lyau-ning** (Manchu-peace).

Note, incidentally, that there are at least three different roots expressing the idea of *peace* (**ping, ning, an**). And you will find other cases where different roots express approximately the same idea. This is usual in any language. We may also mention that the explanation of some meanings is a little complicated; in such cases, we give the place-names without a translation.

The Arrows

The arrows that you see over the Chinese words, represent the tones—level, sharp-rising, deep-rising, falling—and you must disregard them until you have studied **Lesson Five**. That they are important is clear from the fact that two provinces, **Shān-shi** (Mountain-west) and **Shǎn-shi** (Shan-region-west, common spelling *Shensi*), would sound exactly alike except for the tone of their first syllables. On the other hand, if anyone tells you that the Chinese cannot understand you unless you get the tones right, that is an exaggerated fairy tale. The fact is that a lot of foreigners mess up the tones and the Chinese can still guess their meaning. So be practical. Since you can't learn everything at once, leave the tones alone for the present.

Vowel Sounds

Pronounce **hu** and **lu** and **wu** like English *who* and *Lou* and *woo*; all Chinese words spelled with **u** at the end rime with these words and with *shoe, do, Lulu*, etc. Pronounce Chinese **yi** and **ni** like English *ye* and *knee*; all words ending in **i** rime with these and with *be, tea, free*, etc. Pronounce **ba** and **sha** like *bah* and *shah*; all words ending in **a** rime with these and with *pa, ah, tra-la-la*. Examples:

hú	lake	**yi**	one	**bǎ**	eight
lù	road	**shi**	west	**shǎ**	sand
wǔ	five	**nǐ**	you	**tā**	him

   Wú-hú   Wuhu (Weeds-lake)
   Yǎ-lù   Yalu River
   Chá-har   Chahar (named after a Mongol tribe)

When **n** or **ng** are added to **i** or **u** or **a**, the vowel sound may be changed a little bit. **Lin** and **ling** rime with English *win* and *wing*. The word **dung** does not rime with English *rung* nor with any other English word; however, you can get an idea of the sound if you think of it as being *doong*. Chinese **fang** is not like the English word of the same spelling, but instead is like *fa* of the musical scale with *ng* added. Chinese **fan** has a slightly different vowel so that the word seems almost like our English word, but it is undrawled and still keeps a resemblance to the vowel sound of *fa*. Examples:

lín	woods	lún	wheel	fàn	food
líng	range	dūng	east	fàng	put

Djí-lin	Kirin (Lucky-woods)
Nán Líng	South Range
Shǎn-dung	Shantung (Mountain-east)
Kwǎng-dung	Kwangtung or Canton (Broad-east)
Ǎn-ching	Anking (Peace-felicitation)
Nán-djing	Nanking (South-capital)
Hú-nan	Hunan (Lake-south)
Shi-kang	Sikang (West-health)
Djyǎng-shi	Kiangsi (Stream-west)
Djyǎng-su	Kiangsu (named after two cities, Kiang-ning and Suchow)
Gǎn-su	Kansu (named after Kanchow and Suchow)
Shin-djyang	Sinkiang (New-region)
Níng-shyà	Ningsia (Peaceable-Mongol)

The pronunciation of *an* changes when it follows a *y*: it then may rime with English *tan* or possibly even with *ten*. This changed pronunciation explains why some romanizations use *yen* and *ien* for such syllables. The writing **yan** in National Romanization is based on the principle that this is a modification due to the **y** and not a brand-new sound. Chinese people will understand you whether you remember to modify the sound or let it rime with **shan.** Examples:

Myǎn-dyan	Burma
Fú-djyan	Fukien (Named after the cities of Fuchow and Kienyang)
Tyǎn-djin	Tientsin (Heaven-ferry)

Combinations with **y** (as in **tyan, myan,** etc.) are to be pronounced all in one syllable, not as in the English name *Lyons* but like the beginning sound of *mew*. Or take the first two syllables of the phrase *to yonder house*, which we can spell **tu yan** or **tə yan**; run it together into **t'yan** or **tyan** and you have the idea of these syllables.

The pronunciation of **u** is different following **y** in the National Romanization. It is then like the French *u* or the German *ü*, a sound with rounded lips as **u** in **lu** but with the tongue lifted toward the front of the mouth as in pronouncing **i** or **y**. However, in the one combination **yung,** there is no difference in pronunciation and such syllables rime with **dung.** Examples:

Modified **u** (except in the combination **yung**)		Unmodified **u** in **yung,** riming with **dung** (*doong*)	
yú	fish	yùng	use
nyŭ	female	shyúng	bear
chyù	go	shyŭng-dĭ	brothers
yuə̀	month		
yún	clouds		
Yún-nán	Yunnan (Clouds-south)		

The combination **ir** is used for a special sound that has nothing to do with the one in **mi** and **ti.** Our romanized **sir** is a little like the Bostonian pronunciation of *sir*. You can get a reasonably good imitation of the Chinese sound by saying *sir* with the teeth closed together and the point of the tongue held near the roof of the mouth. Note that this sound comes only after **s sh ts ch dz dj.** Examples:

sìr	four	dzìr	written word
shír	ten	djìr	paper
tsìr	stab	Sìr-chwán	Szechwan (Four-stream)
chìr	eat		

Pronounce Chinese **hai** and **tai** like English *high* and *tie*; all syllables ending in **ai** rime with these and with *lye, buy, my, eye*. Pronounce Chinese **hau** like English *how*; all syllables ending in **au** rime with *how, plow, now*. Examples:

hǎi	sea	**hǎu**	good
tài-tai	wife	**dǎu**	island
dài	take along	**yàu**	want
kāi	open	**Lyáu**	Manchu

Shàng-hǎi	Shanghai (Upper-sea)
Chīng-hǎi	Tsinghai (Bluegreen-sea)
Hǎi-nán Dǎu	Hainan Tau (Sea-south Island)
Lyáu-níng	Liaoning (Manchu-peace)

There is a somewhat variable sound in Chinese which the romanizations show sometimes with *e*, sometimes with *o*; we have adopted an inverted ə for the reason that it resembles both letters. The sound is made like the *e* in *let* by many Chinese, but most people say it with the sound in *sun, son, rung* or like what dialect writers show by *uh* in *suh* or *thuh*. The syllable **ər** is like *her* without the *h*; **hə** is like *her* without the *r*; **chəng** rimes with English *rung*. Examples:

ər	two	**dzwə̀**	to do
hə́	river	**djə̀-gə**	this one
wə̌	I	**chə́ng**	city
		mə́n	door, gate

hwə̌-chə̄	train (fire-cart)
Chə́ng-dū	Chengtu
Hwáng Hə́	Yellow River
Hə́-nán	Honan (River-south)

When ə comes after **y**, as in **tyə̌** (iron) or **tyə̌-lù** (railroad [iron-road]) or **shyə̀-shyə** (thanks), the pronunciation is like *yes* without the final sound.

Pronounce **bəi** and **həi** like English *bay* and *hay*, and all other syllables ending in **əi** to rime with these and with *weigh*, *sleigh*, *they*, etc. Pronounce **djəu** like English *Joe* and all words in **əu** to rime with these and with *go*, *low*, *know*, *toe*, *dough*; the common spelling for this sound is *ow*, as in Fuchow, Hankow, etc. Examples:

bə̌i	north	**djəu**	region
gwə̌i	honored	**kə̌u**	mouth

Bə̌i-píng	Peiping (North-peace)
Bə̌i-djing	Peking (North-capital)
Hə́-bə̌i	Hopei (River-north)
Wə́i-hə̌i-wə̀i	Weihaiwei (Majestic-sea-guard)
Hə̌i-lung-djyang	Heilungkiang (Black-dragon-stream, Chinese name for the Amur River and the province bordering it)
Gwə̀i-lín	Kweilin (Honored-woods)
Gwə̀i-djəu	Kweichow (Honored-region)
Hwə̀i-djəu	Hweichow (Excellent-region)
Sü-djəu	Suchow in Kiangsu province (Cheerful-region)
Sù-djəu	Suchow in Kansu province (Respectful-region)
Fú-djəu	Fuchow
Hàn-kə̌u	Hankow (Han-mouth, that is mouth of the Han River)

LEARNING TIP 1: IMITATE

The way to guarantee that you will be understood when you talk Chinese, is to use the same sounds, tone, and rhythm as the people themselves. And the best way to learn this is by ear and imitation. At your earliest opportunity, get a Chinese to say aloud the words and sentences you are learning, and repeat after him. Thruout this book, you will find suggestions to carry out with 'your Chinese speaker.' This assumes that sooner or later you will be in contact with Chinese-speaking people. Whenever you are, you can carry out any practice you have missed earlier.

There is no harm, however, in speaking less than perfectly at the outset. All learning is by trial and error; that is, you make a stab at the thing, see how you're doing, and then improve on it. If you are generally disposed to listen to the way people talk and to imitate them, and if you take particular note every time they seem to have trouble catching your words, you have a good chance of ending up with a fairly native-sounding accent.

DO THIS: As soon as you have a Chinese speaker to help you, go thru all the examples in this lesson. Let him say each word or expression aloud a couple of times with you repeating after him each time. If two times isn't enough, give it whatever it needs.

You may find that some things are harder than others. The Chinese speaker will let you know if you are getting the idea, and you must try to say things in a way that seems all right to him. However, if there is some little point you fail to get, don't wear yourself and your friend out with it. Skip it for the time being and come back to it later after you have had more opportunity to hear the language spoken.

If you have no one to help you at first, at least make it a point to read the examples out loud two or more times each.

TEST YOURSELF

1. Here are a few miscellaneous items, in English, but spelled in the manner of the Chinese National Romanization. Where an English sound doesn't exist in Chinese, we use the next closest sound. If you read the items out loud,

you should be able to understand them, and you will find
this good practice for getting used to the romanization.

(a) Dəu, rəi, mi, fa, səu, la, ti, dəu.

(b) Wən, tu, tri, fər, faiv, siks, səvən, əit, nain, tən.

(c) Sim-pəl Sai-mən mət ə pai-mən,
  Gəu-ying tu də fər.
Səd Sim-pəl Sai-mən tu də pai-mən,
  Lət mi təist yur wər.
Səd də pai-mən tu sim-pəl Sai-mən,
  Lət mi si yur pə-ni.
Səd Sim-pəl Sai-mən tu də pai-mən,
  In-did Ai hav nat ə-ni.

2. Here is a make-believe map, using geographic words
we have run across in this Session. Read the words aloud to
test your ability to get the sounds from the spelling. If there
is any point you are not clear about, re-read the paragraph
that explains it.

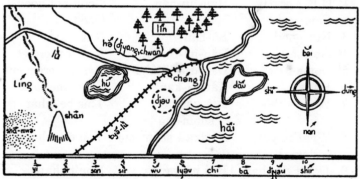

3. Assuming that you have spent several minutes studying the map of the Chinese provinces on page xviii, see how
many of the provinces you can now name from memory.
Afterwards, check back and note the ones you missed.

EXPRESSIONS FOR GETTING ALONG

SECOND SESSION
SEVENTEEN SENTENCES

Here are seventeen Chinese sentences which will get you just about anything you want, provided you use them cleverly and throw in a few gestures.

English	Chinese	Word-by-word
1. O.K.? *or* Hi!	Hǎu-bu-hǎu	Good-not-good
2. Fine, good	Hǎu	Good
3. Not good	Bù-hǎu	Not-good
4. Go there	Dàu-nǎ-li chyù	Reach-there go
5. Come here	Dàu-djə̀-li lái	Reach-here come
6. Have a look	Kàn-yi-kan	Look-one-look
7. What's this?	Djə̀-gə shìr shə́m-mə	This be what
8. What're you doing?	Nǐ dzwə̀ shə́m-mə	You do what
9. Don't do that	Byə́ nà-yang	Don't that-manner
10. Do this	Dzwə̀ djə̀-yang	Do this-manner
11. I want this one	Wǒ-yàu djə̀-gə	I-want this-item
12. Give me that one	Gə́i-wǒ nà-gə	Give-me that-item

10

13. How much money?	Dwə̄-shǎu chyán	Much-little-money
14. Where's Peiping?	Bə̌i-píng dzài-shə́m-mə dǐ-fang	Peiping located-what place
15. You take me —O.K.?	Nǐ dài-wə̌ chyù —hǎu-bu-hǎu	You lead-me go —good-not-good
16. Thanks	Shyə̀-shyə	Thank-thank
17. So long	Dzài-djyàn	Again-see

LEARNING TIP 2: READ, SPEAK, LISTEN

When you come to a new Chinese expression, read it out loud. In that way it hits three of your senses: (1) your eye sees it, (2) the muscles of your lips, tongue, etc. have the feel of producing it, and (3) your ear hears it. In this way the impression is fuller and stronger and you have a better chance of remembering the expression when you need to use it. In fact, it is a good idea to say each Chinese word or phrase out loud at least twice whenever you come to it in reading.

Don't be surprised if you sometimes seem to forget expressions almost as fast as you learn them. Chinese is not like French or Spanish or Dutch, where half the words are at least partly similar to the English. As a result you have to use a word twenty to fifty times before it sticks with you. It's easy to keep up your practice if you are in a place where you speak Chinese every day. Otherwise, you have to make up for it by reviewing.

DO THIS: Before you read on, go thru the entire list of sentences two or three times, reading the English and the Chinese out loud.

If you have a Chinese speaker, do it this way: (1) you read the English; (2) the Chinese speaker says the Chinese loud and clear, (3) you repeat after him, (4) the speaker says it again, (5) you repeat a second time. If the book is used in a class or in a study group, the teacher or leader of the group should read the English, followed by the Chinese speaker and then the whole class chiming in.

Explanations

Point 1. The word **hǎu** means *good* or *O.K.* **Bù-hǎu** is *not-good*. Combining both expressions into **hǎu-bu-hǎu** is like saying *Good or not good*, which is the Chinese way of asking *Is it O.K.?* This is about the most useful phrase in the language. You can use it for *Hello* or *Hi* (sentence 1) or as a way of showing you mean to be polite about a request, as in sentence 15, where *You take me—O.K.?* is the same as saying *How about taking me there?* or *Please guide me.*

You can also use **hǎu-bu-hǎu** to ask permission. For instance, the following is like saying *Is it O.K. for me to have a look?*

I'll have a look —O.K.?	**Wǒ kàn-yi-kan —hǎu-bu-hǎu**	I look-one-look— good-not-good

Combine *good* with *look* and you get *good-looking*:

This one's pretty, that one's ugly	**Djə̀-gə hǎu-kàn, nà-gə bù-hǎu-kàn**	This good-look, that not-good-look

In the phrase **díng-hǎu,** which you hear so often, the word **dǐng** means *roof* or *top* or *most.* The general idea is *top-good* or *tops!*

Point 2. To say *is it good?* you say *good-not-good.* The same system is used for other questions. Examples:

Do you want?	**Nǐ yàu-bu-yàu**	You want-not-want
Is it so? ·	**Shìr-bu-shìr**	Be-not-be
Are you looking?	**Nǐ kàn-bu-kàn**	You look-not-look
Are you coming?	**Nǐ lái-bu-lái**	You come-not-come
Are you going?	**Nǐ chyù-bu-chyù**	You go-not-go
Will you get there?	**Nǐ dàu-bu-dàu**	You reach-not-reach

On the same principle you say *much-little* for *how much?* (**dwǒ-shǎu**), as in sentence 13. It's like asking *is it much or little?*

However, if there is a word like *what* or *who* or *where* in the sentence, that is to say, a word that is a question in itself, then your question is complete in the simple form. Examples:

What's this?	**Djè shìr shém-mə**	This be what
What do you want?	**Nǐ yàu shém-mə**	You want what
What're you doing?	**Nǐ dzwò shém-mə**	You do what
What're you looking at?	**Nǐ kàn shém-mə**	You look what
Where's Peiping?	**Běi-píng dzài-shém-mə dì-fang**	Peiping located-what-place
Where are you?	**Nǐ dzài-shém-mə-dì-fang**	You located-what-place
Where are you going?	**Nǐ dàu-shém-mə-dì-fang chyu**	You reach-what-place go

Use a question-word with an expression like *want-not-want* and the question-word changes its meaning; for example:

| Do you want any-thing? | Nǐ yàu-bu-yàu shə́m-mə | You want-not-want what |
| Do you do any-thing? | Nǐ dzwə̀-bu-dzwə̀ shə́m-mə | You do-not-do what |

Point 3. There are no words for *yes* and *no* in Chinese. If they ask *do you want* (yàu-bu-yàu), you answer either *want* (yàu) or *not-want* (bú-yàu). If they say *are you doing it?* (nǐ dzwə̀-bu-dzwə̀), your answer is either *do* (dzwə̀) or *not-do* (bú-dzwə̀). It's simple enough, but if you get stuck, you can always get by with one of the following four expressions, which are therefore well worth memorizing:

O. K.	Hǎu	Good
Not O. K.	Bù-hǎu	Not-good
It's so	Shìr	Be
It isn't so	Bú-shìr	Not-be

LEARNING TIP 3: USE YOUR HEAD

Use your head to figure out ways of getting your meaning across with what few words you know. For example, you go to a Chinese mechanic to get your brakes fixed. You say, *Hi, come here, have a look.* When he comes over, work your brake and say, *Not O.K.*

If you follow this system you will not only get what you want but you will also be using the same words over and over till they stick with you. In the end you learn the language a lot faster than the man who is always thumbing thru his dictionary to find the exact translation of his thoughts.

PRACTICAL TEST

What can you do in the practical situations described below? Look for a suitable sentence among the seventeen at the beginning of this Session, or, if you can, do it from memory. Anyhow, say the Chinese out loud with gestures.

1. You go into a silk store to look around. What do you say for *Hello?*

2. The clerk answers your greeting by saying, **Hǎu, shyè-shyə. Ní hǎu-bu-hǎu.** What is she saying? How do you answer?

3. How do you ask permission to look around?

4. You see some handkerchiefs and want to know the price for six. What do you say and what do you do?

5. The clerk holds up two $500 bills (Chinese money) to show the price. You don't want to pay that much. How do you tell her so?

6. You want to offer $500. What do you say and do?

7. You settle on $800. Hand her the money and ask if it's right?

8. She answers, **Hǎu. Shyè-shyə.** Then she shows you a dressing gown. Tell her you don't care for it.

9. You notice that the clerk is wearing a beautiful scarf. How do you find out if she'll sell?

10. She doesn't want to sell. Instead she goes to the showcase and says, **Dàu-djè-li lái kàn-yi-kan.** What does that mean?

11. She shows you another scarf. Can you understand her if she says, **Djè-gə hǎu-kàn. Ní yǎu-bu-yǎu.**

12. You finish shopping. Tell the girl thanks and good-by.

THIRD SESSION
HOW THEY'RE BUILT

If you know how the sentences are put together and what each word means, you will be able to say a lot of new things with the same words. Study the Word-by-word breakdown (third column) of the Seventeen Sentences. Then read the following explanations.

Point 4. In Chinese, as in any other language, there are words that sound exactly like other words. English examples are seen in: 'Don't hide my nail file in the letter file,' 'Blackberries are green when they are red,' 'When the light blue fly came to light on the electric light, I gave it a light blow with a light sledgehammer.' Chinese examples in our Seventeen Sentences are:

> **dzài** meaning both *again* and *located*
> **dzwò** meaning both *sit* and *do, make*
> **shìr** meaning both *be* and *job, work, matter*

As in English, you can tell what is meant by the way the word is used. Can you translate the following:

Wǒ dzài-djò-li dzwò   **Djò-gə bú-shìr Běi-píng**
Wǒ bú-yàu dzài chyù   **Wǒ bú-yàu dzwò shìr**

There are also words that sound alike at first, but are absolutely different once you get used to Chinese tones. This will be discussed later.

Point 5. Notice the following sets of words:

this	**djò**		that	**nà**
this one	**djò-gə**		that one	**nà-gə**

like this	**djə̀-yang**	like that	**nà-yang**
this place	**djə̀-gə dì-fang**	that place	**nà-gə dì-fang**
here	**djə̀-li**	there	**nà-li**

The simple word **djə̀** is used mostly when you mean *this stuff* or *this situation* or *this matter*. **Djə̀-gə** is used to refer to a specific person or thing; note that to say *this place* you use **djə̀-gə dì-fang**, which is like saying *this-item place*. For *like this* or *in this way* you say **djə̀-yang**, which may be translated *this-manner*. For *it is here*, you can use *located-this-item place* (**dzài-djə̀-gə dì-fang**) or *located-here* (**dzài-djə̀-li**). Note that the words for *here* and *there* are made up with the words for *this* and *that* with an added syllable, which means *in*; that is to say, **djə̀-li** for *here* is made up of *this-in* and **nà-li** for *there* is made up of *that-in*.

For saying *don't do that* (sentence 9), the most common expression is *don't that-manner*; the word for *do* can be put in but it is not usual. The shorter expression is like saying *not that way* in English.

The Chinese of Peiping use slightly different demonstratives from those listed above: this **djə̀i**, this one **djə̀i-gə**, here **djə̀r**; that **nə̀i**, that one **nə̀i-gə**, there **nə̀r**. The greater number of Chinese say **djə̀** etc., but Peiping is the foremost Mandarin-speaking city. So you can take your choice.

Point 6. Chinese sentences are worded much like our telegrams. In general, things that can be easily guessed are left out. A waiter is likely to say *Want-what?* (**yàu-shəm-mə**) without bringing in the word for *you*, since anyone can see he's talking to you. When you answer, it's enough to say *Want beans* rather than *I want beans*, because he will understand you aren't ordering for your uncle back in Rhode Island. On the other hand, if there are two of you each ordering something different, then you'd say:

I want this,	**Wǒ yàu djə̀-gə,**	I want this,
he wants that	**tā yàu nà-gə**	he want that

Point 7. These words are important to know:

me *or* I	**wǒ**	us *or* we	**wǒ-mən**
you (one person)	**nǐ**	you people	**nǐ-mən**
him *or* he	**tā**	them *or* they	**tā-mən**
her *or* she	**tā**		
it	**tā**		

Notice that in Chinese the word for *you* is different according to whether you are talking to one person or to more than one. Otherwise, the words of this set (the pronouns) are simpler in Chinese than in English. Single words go for *me* or *I*, for *us* or *we*, for *them* or *they*. And the word **tā** goes for male or female or object.

Point 8. Study the following expressions, which the Chinese language makes with a clever use of the word for *one:*

Have a look	**Kàn-yi-kan**	Look-one-look
Go for a little while	**Chyù-yi-chyu**	Go-one-go
Sit a while	**Dzwə̀-yi-dzwə**	Sit-one-sit

Point 9. The word for *want* is good to know in any language. Study the following examples, which show different ways of using the word **yàu**, meaning *want* or *will:*

Do you want?	**Nǐ yàu-bu-yàu**	You want-not-want
I want that	**Wǒ yàu nà-gə**	I want that
I want to go *or* I'll go	**Wǒ yàu-chyù**	I want-go
I want you to come	**Wǒ yàu nǐ-lái**	I want you-come

Point 10. For telling a person not to do something you can say *not-want,* which is like telling him he doesn't want to do it, or you can use the simplified form **byò,** which we translate *don't.* The short expression is the more usual.

Don't go   **Byò-chyù** *or* **bú-yàu chyù**

LEARNING TIP 4: USE CHINESE MODELS

Never try to make up sentences in English and then translate them word-for-word into Chinese. If you do, you get stuff that sounds as puzzling and odd as the things we sometimes hear foreigners say in English. Instead, make all new sentences on the model of the Chinese sentences you already know. For example, taking the model of sentence 14, *Where's Peiping?* you can make:

Where's Shanghai?	**Shàng-hǎi dzài-shòm-mə-dǐ-fang**	Shanghai located-what-place
Where's the coffee?	**Kā-fēi dzài-shòm-mə-dǐ-fang**	Coffee located-what-place
Where is he?	**Tā dzài-shòm-mə-dǐ-fang**	He located-what-place
The coffee's there	**Kā-fēi dzài-nà-li**	Coffee located-there
He's here	**Tā dzài-djò-li**	He located-here
He's in Peiping	**Tā dzài-Bòi-píng**	He located-Peiping

You see that sentence 14 is made up of two parts, the word *Peiping* and the expression that refers to its location *(located-what-place).* Instead of *Peiping,* you can use the name of any place or person or object. And instead of *located-what-place* you can say *located-there, located-here* or located any place you wish. Using this model you can make hundreds of sentences, all of them perfect Chinese.

In the same way you can make plenty of good sentences using the model of sentence 7, *This be what?* For example:

What is he?	**Tă shìr shǒm-mə**	He be-what
That's Peiping	**Nǎ shìr Bǒi-píng**	That be Peiping

DO THIS: Go over the Seventeen Sentences with your Chinese speaker once more, following the same method as before. Keep trying your best to mimic his tone and rhythm as well as the sounds.

PRACTICAL TEST

Pick out the right answer from the phonies and speak it out loud with gestures.

1. Seeing a friend in a restaurant, you walk up and say:
(A) **Shyà-shyə.** (B) **Shìr-bu-shìr.** (C) **Hă021u-bu-hău.**

2. Your friend answers:
(A) **Wǒ-hău, ní hău-bu-hău.** (B) **Dzài-djyàn.** (C) **Nǐ bu-hău-kàn.**

3. She invites you to sit:
(A) **Nǐ lái dzwò, hău-bu-hău.** (B) **Wǒ bu-yàu nǐ chyù.**
(C) **Dzwò djǒ-yang.**

4. You thank her:
(A) **Dzài-shǒm-mə dì-fang.** (B) **Shyà-shyə.** (C) **Tă bù-hău.**

5. The waiter comes and asks what you'll have:
(A) **Nǐ yàu-bu-yàu lái.** (B) **Nà-gə shìr shǒm-mə.** (C) **Nǐ yàu shǒm-mə.**

6. Wishing to order what your friend has, you point and say:
(A) **Gǒi-tă nà-gə.** (B) **Yàu nà-gə.** (C) **Yàu kàn-yi-kan.**

7. The waiter asks how you like the food:
(A) **Dwə̄-shǎu chyán.** (B) **Hǎu-bu-hǎu.** (C) **Dzwə̀-yi-dzwə.**

8. It's delicious, so you say:
(A) **Dzài-djə̀-li.** (B) **Djə̀-gə shìr shə́m-mə.** (C) **Díng-hǎu.**

9. You order coffee for the two of you:
(A) **Gə́i-wə̌ kā-fə̄i.** (B) **Gə́i-wə̌-mən kā-fə̄i.** (C) **Shìr-bu-shìr kā-fə̄i.**

10. You ask for the bill:
(A) **Wə̌-yǎu-chyù.** (B) **Dwə̄-shǎu chyán.** (C) **Wə̌ bú-yǎu gə̌i chyán.** (D) **Byə̀ djə̀-yang.**

11. You and your friend say good-by to the waiter:
(A) **Dzài-djyàn.** (B) **Nǐ dǎi-wə̌-mən lái.** (C) **Nǐ-mən dǎu-nǎ-li chyu.**

FOURTH SESSION
CLINCHING THEM

By now you are pretty familiar with the expressions in the Seventeen Sentences. It is therefore a good time to try to clinch them in your mind, so you will know them thoroly and be able to use them at any time without stopping to think.

The Cover-Up Method

Cover up the English columns. Read the Chinese aloud and see if you can give the meaning. When you come to one you don't know, look at the English. Having got the meaning, go on to the next expression and the next till you finish. Go thru the entire list again and again until you can do the whole of it without missing.

Then cover up the Chinese and see if you can give it for

each English expression. Always say the Chinese out loud.

DO THIS: Take time out right now, at least fifteen or twenty minutes, to work over the expressions using the memory system just described. After that, go thru all the expressions once more with your Chinese speaker, but this time without looking in the book and without saying the English.

LEARNING TIP 5: MEMORY AIDS

When you're trying to learn words in a new language, it's sometimes helpful to think of some English word whose sound and meaning remind you of the foreign word. For example:

Kids *yowl* for castoria.   (**Yàu** means *want*.)
This is a *jugga* cida.   (**Djə̀-gə** means *this*.)
Chyu-zit, da cops!   (**Chyù** means *go*.)
We *conn* the sea from a *conn*ing tower.   (**Kàn** means *look*.)
Gə̌i means *give* or *gave* as in *gi*mme and *ga'e*me.
Sure, it is.   (**Shìr** means *it is*.)

You can make up silly phrases for any word you especially want to remember. After you've used the word a few times and know it well you can forget the memory aid. You don't want too many trick phrases in your mind because then you can't keep them apart.

LEARNING TIP 6: SPEAK UP

Memorizing words is one thing, speaking a language is another. You must get so that the words **díng-hǎu** or **wǒ yàu nǎ-gə** just naturally come to your mind every time you see something nice. The way to get a direct-fire memory is by using the expressions often in natural situations. Be friendly and talkative. Try to say something every time you meet Chinese people. This will be much easier later on when you learn a few more expressions.

The Practical Dictionary

The short Practical Dictionary at the back of this book contains only the most common ordinary words. It has been kept short not to save space, but so you will use the words again and again until you know them well, instead of scattering your attention over thousands of different words. Look for *help* and not for *assist*, for *big* and not for *colossal*. If you don't find what you want, think of some other way of putting the idea.

PRACTICAL TEST

In this test don't look up more than one word for each problem. Follow Chinese models you know, fitting the new word into the proper place. Your answer is correct if you can be understood by a Chinese.

1. Taking a friend to supper, you ask, *Is this restaurant O.K.?*
2. Order rice.
3. Order beef.
4. Order tea.
5. Ask your friend if she likes the meat.
6. Ask her to pass the salt.
7. Ask her if she'd care to go to the movies.
8. When you see her home, ask for a kiss.
9. She says: **Byó nǎ-yang.** What does that mean?
10. The rest is up to you. Don't look up too many words,

ON THE SOUNDS, CONTINUED

FIFTH SESSION

THE TONES

If you learn to speak Chinese like the people themselves, they will like you for it and they will understand you better. If you have followed instructions about listening to Chinese speakers and imitating them, you must by now have a reasonably good and understandable pronunciation. This Session and the ninth give you drill on points that need special attention.

The tones of Chinese aren't as hard as some people make out. Actually there is no tone in Chinese that we don't also have in English. The difference is that in English we use different tones to show whether we are asking a question or making a statement. In Chinese each syllable has its own tone which stays put regardless of whether you are asking or telling.

1. *Level tone.* Like sounding *Mi-mi-mi*
tā yī sān chyǎn shïr (him, one, three, thousand, army division)

2. *Sharp-rising tone.* Like asking in English: *Huh? huh?*
lái chá rén chyán shír (come, tea, person, money, ten)

3. *Deep-rising tone.* When someone is telling a story, you say *yeah, yeah* to show you want him to go on. Drag it out.
hǎu wǒ nǐ chyǎn shïr (good, me, you, shallow, dung)

24

4. *Falling tone.* Like an abrupt command; say: *Don't!*
Don't!
dzài kàn yàu chyàn shìr (located, look, want, owe, be)

5. *Four tones.* Words that are alike as to sounds and different as to tones, may seem entirely alike at first but not after you get used to Chinese. It isn't at all hard to distinguish the sound of **mài** with falling tone, which means *sell*, and **mài** with deep-rising tone, which means *buy*. The same goes for the examples given below. First say your English examples, then hum them, then say the Chinese—each twice.

(English examples)

mi   mi   huh?   huh?   yeah,   yeah,   don't!   don't!

♩   ♩   ♫   ♫   ♩♪   ♩♪   ♩   ♩

hm   hm   hm   hm   hmm   hmm   hm   hm
(hum to get the sound)

shìr shìr shír shír shìr shìr shìr shìr
(division, ten, dung, be)
chyǎn chyǎn chyán chyán chyǎn chyǎn chyàn chyàn
(thousand, money, shallow, owe)

6. *Weak Syllables.* In some words there is a second syllable that is very short and weak and whose tone is middle or low in pitch. Examples:

yā-dz dāu-dz dūng-shi tā-də (duck, knife, thing, his)
yí-dz lán-dz húng-də wán-lə (soap, basket, red, finished)
yǐ-dz tǎn-dz nǐ-də hǎu-lə (chair, blanket, yours, repaired)
kù-dz dàu-dz djè-gə hwài-lə (pants, mature rice, this, spoiled)

Words like **yā-dz** etc. should properly be spelled **yā-dzir**; that is, they have the vowel sound described on p. 5. However, in the weak syllable, the effect is like the *dz* of *adze* pronounced with an extra push to the ending.

7. *Simplification of deep-rising.* When a deep-rising syllable is followed by another syllable, as in the examples of the third set in 6, you pronounce a deep tone but don't rise on the same syllable. You hold the deep tone till you get to the second syllable which is on a higher pitch. The two syllables together sound something like our *uh-huh* when used in place of *yeah* to get a person to go on with his story.

Compare the word **yĭ-dz** (chair) with **yí-dz** (soap). The combination of a deep tone followed by a weak syllable on the higher pitch is very different from the sharp-rising tone followed by the middle-pitched weak syllable.

8. *Change of deep-rising.* You may have noticed that deep-rising tones sometimes change to sharp-rising, for instance, *give* is **gˇ̌i** but *give-me* is **gˊi-wˇ̌**. This happens with deep-rising syllables every time they are followed by another deep-rising syllable in the same phrase, that is, when they are pronounced together without any pause. Examples:

Give-me	**Gˊi-wˇ̌**	**Gˇ̌i + wˇ̌**
You-O.K.	**Nˊi-hǎu**	**Nˇ̌i + hǎu**
I-O.K.	**Wˊ̌-hǎu**	**Wˇ̌ + hǎu**

9. *Tone-weakening.* Chinese words, like English, often lose their original accent when they are put into sentences. They may keep a light accent, with the tone less clearly spoken but still recognizable, or they may become weak syllables, like those described under 6.

10. *Rhythm.* The best way to get a good easy pronunciation is to get the rhythm of the whole sentence. Instead of speaking one syllable at a time, learn to speak in natural groups.

DO THIS: Go thru all the examples, with your Chinese speaker. He should say all the examples in a set, not one at a time, so you can get a real impression of the sound. Then you repeat the whole set. If there are several of you, it is a good idea to do the exercises in chorus and then individually. This is so the Chinese speaker can hear your pronunciation and correct you if necessary.

If you have no Chinese speaker, get what you can out of the explanation and skip to the next session.

DICTATION

You will find it helps your feeling for Chinese sounds quite a bit if you try to write down words and phrases you hear. Have your Chinese speaker dictate some words taken from the exercises in mixed order. Write them and then check to see what you've missed. Concentrate on the tones this time.

Try to use the same kind of spelling as we use in this book. That way you'll learn more quickly to read the words in the Practical Dictionary with the right pronunciation.

English and Chinese use the same tones

EVERYDAY CONVERSATION

SIXTH SESSION
CONVERSATIONAL EXPRESSIONS

Trying to talk pidgin English will help give you the feel of how Chinese sentences are built. After this we will give the word-by-word equivalent of the Chinese in the first column. When it's hard to guess the real meaning, we add it in parentheses.

Reach-what-place go (Where are you going?)	Dằu-shớm-mə-dǐ-fang chyu
Not-reach-what-place go (Not going anywhere)	Bú-dằu-shớm-mə-dǐ-fang chyu
You called what?	Nǐ djyằu shớm-mə
I be Lee-Mr. (I am Mr. Lee)	Wớ shǐr Lǐ-Shyan-shəng
You-howabout? (How about you?)	Nǐ-nə
You be what-place-belonging person (Where are you from?)	Nǐ shǐr shớm-mə-dǐ-fang-də rớn
Be China-person, be America-person (Are you Chinese or American?)	Shǐr Djüng-gwə-rən, shǐr Mới-gwə-rən
You located-what-place live	Nǐ dzằi-shớm-mə-dǐ-fang djù
Have-haven't wife (Are you married or single?)	Yớu-məi-yớu tằi-tai

Have	Yŏu
Haven't	Mǎi-yŏu
Husband, *also* Mr., gentleman, teacher	Shyǎn-shəng
Child	Hái-dz
You-belonging father still located-not-located (Is your father still alive?)	Nǐ-də fù-chin hái dzài-budzài
Located (He's living)	Dzài
Not-located-done (He passed away)	Bú-dzài-lə
Mother	Mǔ-chin
You do what job (What's your trade?)	Nǐ dzwờ shǎm-mə shr̀
Not-do what job (I have no work)	Bú-dzwờ shǎm-mə shr̀
I not-understand	Wŏ bù-dǔng
Again-speak one-time (Repeat)	Dzài-shwờ yí-tsr̀
You be-not-be soldier	Nǐ shr̀-bu-shr̀ bing
Work-person-huh? (Are you a worker?)	Gǔng-rən-ma
Buy-sell-person	Mǎi-mai-rən

LEARNING TIP 7: REPEAT NEW WORDS

When someone is speaking to you and uses a word you don't understand, repeat it after him once or several times. This gives you time to think; sometimes you remember the word while saying it over. It also gives you pronunciation practice and helps you learn words. Besides, it makes the man realize you are just learning the language, so he may speak more slowly and use simpler words.

LEARNING TIP 8: KEEP SMILING

In making conversation, it doesn't hurt to ask silly questions as a friendly joke. For instance, you can ask a Chinese school-kid if he's American, then if he has a wife, and when he says *No*, ask if he has children.

LEARNING TIP 9: TWO-WAY QUESTIONS

Whenever you hear something you don't understand, you can make a guess as to what it's about and ask, *Is it or isn't it such-and-such?* For instance, if you know a man is trying to tell you his trade, you can say *You be-not-be mechanic, You be-not-be driver* and so forth. He will answer **Bú-shìr** (not-be) until you hit the right one and then he'll say **Shìr** (be).

Guessing is always a big help toward understanding. If you know more or less what a man is talking about, it's easier to recognize words you know and to piece together half-understood sentences. It is specially helpful when you're having trouble catching the man's pronunciation. Also don't forget to use gestures and rough pencil sketches as well as words.

PRACTICAL TEST

Ask your Chinese speaker the questions given at the beginning of this Session and see if you can understand his answers. Then let him ask while you answer.

SEVENTH SESSION
HOW THEY'RE BUILT

DO THIS: Spend about 10 minutes practicing the tone exercises of the Fifth Session. Then run thru the conversational sentences in the Sixth Session.

Explanations

Point 11. The word **djyǎu** for *called* or *call* can be used of anything, an object or a person or a place or a word.

This called what?	**Djə̀-gə djyǎu shə́m-mə**
You called what?	**Nǐ djyǎu shə́m-mə**
This you-folks call what (What do you call this?)	**Djə̀-gə nǐ-mən djyǎu shə́m-mə**
Here called what?	**Djə̀-li djyǎu shə́m-mə**
Truck called what?	*Truck* **djyǎu shə́m-mə**

In polite conversation, there's a fancier way of asking a person's name. They say *Honorable-name* and you answer *Humble-name Winterbotham.* This phrase is in the Dictionary under *Honorable* but you'd better use the simple expression for now.

Point 12. Chinese for *Mr. Lee* is *Lee-Mr.* (**Lǐ-Shyan-shəng**), that is, the *Mr.* comes after the name. In the same way, you say *Lee-Mrs.* and *Lee-Miss.* These words are in the Practical Dictionary.

The word **shyǎn-shəng** can be broken down to *first-born.* Since there is nothing about man in it, it is not surprising that it is used also for a *teacher* of either sex.

Point 13. Chinese has a few small words that are never

used alone but are always tacked on to other words. The
most important one is **də**, which is like our *'s* but used in
various ways. We can take *belonging* as a rough translation.
Study the examples:

Here-belonging person	**Djə̀-li-də rə́n**
(Natives of this place)	
Us-belonging job (Our job)	**Wə̆-mən-də shìr**
This be him-belonging	**Djə̀-gə shir tă-də**
(This is his)	
That be soldier-belonging	**Nă-gə shìr bing-də**
(That is a soldier's)	
Me-belonging be good-	**Wə̆-də shìr hău-də**
belonging (Mine is a good one)	
Buy-sell-belonging (Business)	**Măi-măi-də**
He-speak-belonging good	**Tă-shwə̆-də hău**
(His speaking's good, he	
speaks well)	
Do-job-belonging person	**Dzwə̀-shìr-də rə́n**
(People who work)	

Point 14. Tacked-on **ma** is like a question mark that you
speak out loud. We can translate it as *huh?*

You-good-huh?	**Ní-hău-ma**
Me-huh? (Do you mean me?)	**Wə̆-ma**
Located-here-huh? (Is it here?)	**Dzài-djə̀-li-ma**

Hău-ma has about the same meaning as **hău-bu-hău**, so
that **ma** is just another way of asking a question. Expressions like **hău-bu-hău** are considered a clearer way of speaking, but the expression with **ma** is preferred in cases like
Dzài-djə̀-li-ma rather than the long phrase **Dzài-bu-dzài-
djə̀-li.**

Point 15. Tacked-on **nə** can be translated *how about?* but it is used at the end instead of the beginning. Examples:

Him-howabout (How about him?)	**Tă-nə**
Soldier-howabout (How about the soldiers?)	**Bîng-nə**
Me-belonging-howabout (How about mine?)	**Wŏ-də-nə**

Point 16. Tacked-on **lə** is used in different ways. Often it shows that a thing has happened in the past.

I come-done (I've come)	**Wŏ lái-lə**
We reach-done (We've arrived)	**Wŏ-mən dău-lə**
Him do-done (He's done it)	**Tă dzwò-lə**

Sometimes **lə** gives a special meaning which doesn't have to be connected with having done the thing in the past. With some words, **lə** is dropped for the negative and question forms.

Not-located-done (Pass away)	**Bú-dzài-lə**
Correct, not-correct, correct-not-correct	**Dwài-lə, bú-dwài, dwài-bu-dwài**

Point 17. Since *have* is **yŏu**, you'd expect **bù-yŏu** for *haven't.* But the Mandarin expression happens to be **méi-yŏu** and the phrase with **bu** is generally regarded as baby-talk— like saying *foots* instead of *feet* in English.

Haven't wife	**Méi-yŏu tài-tai**
Have-haven't child	**Yŏu-méi-yŏu hái-dz**
He haven't go (He hasn't gone)	**Tă méi-yŏu chyù**
Go-done haven't go (Has he gone or hasn't he?)	**Chyù-lə méi-yəu chyù**
Go-done haven't (same idea)	**Chyù-lə méi-yŏu**

Notice that you use a tacked-on lǝ to speak of something that has been done but the separate word **méi-yǒu** for what hasn't been.

Point 18. One use of **yǒu** and **méi-yǒu** is to state whether a given object is or is not in a given place. The meaning is about like *there is, there are.*

Here have soldier (There are   **Djè-li yǒu bīng**
    soldiers here)

Point 19. In Chinese, one word goes both for *soldier* and *soldiers*, one for *person* and *people* and so forth. You judge from the situation which fits. When you need to be specific, you use the word for *one* if it's only one and words like *several, many* or *all* if there are more than one.

Point 20. The word for *still* (**hái**) sounds exactly like the root-syllable of *child* (**hái-dz**). Note the similarity but don't let it confuse you. It's no worse than the English sentence, *He owns a still but is still sober.*

In some parts of China, the word **hái-dz** means *shoe* as well as *child.* In these parts people are confused unless you say *small* with *child* (**shyǎu-hái-dz**) and specify *leather-shoe* (**pí-hái**) or *cloth-shoe* (**bù-hái**) for *shoes.*

PRACTICAL TEST

Here is a conversation between two men who meet walking along the road. For each question pick out the sensible answer.

1. **Ní hǎu-bu-hǎu.**
(A) **Nǐ-dǝ hǎu.** (B) **Nǐ bu-hǎu.** (C) **Dǐng-hǎu, nǐ-nǝ.**
2. **Dàu-shém-mǝ dì-fang chyù.**
(A) **Dàu-Běi-píng.** (B) **Dzài-Běi-píng.** (C) **Shìr Shàng-hǎi-rǝn.**

3. Nǐ yàu-dzwò shém-mə.
(A) Bu-dàu-shém-mə dì-fang chyù. (B) Wǒ-yàu kàn-yi-kan.
(C) Yǒu tài-tai, yǒu hái-dz.

4. Wǒ bu-dǔng, dzài shwō.
(A) Wǒ-yàu kàn-yi-kan. (B) Dzài-djyàn. (C) Dǔng-bu-dǔng.

5. Nǐ shìr shém-mə dì-fang-də rén.
(A) Shìr bìng. (B) Dzwò-shìr-də rén. (C) Měi-gwə-rén.

6. Nǐ dzài-shém-mə dì-fang djù.
(A) Dàu-*Waco*-ma. (B) Byé dzwò nà-gə. (C) Dzài-djè-li.

7. Nǐ-də fù-chin hái dzài-bu-dzài.
(A) Nǐ-də-na. (B) Dzài. (C) Dwò-shǎu chyán.

8. Nǐ-də mǔ-chin-na.
(A) Bu-dzài-lə. (B) Shyè-shyə. (C) Tā měi-yǒu hái-dz.

9. Nǐ yǒu-məi-yǒu tài-tai.
(A) Yǒu. (B) Tā-mən yǒu. (C) Géi-wǒ nà-gə.

10. Hái-dz-na.
(A) Dài-wǒ-mən chyù. (B) Měi-yǒu chyù. (C) Hái měi-yǒu.

11. Nǐ dzwò shém-mə shìr.
(A) Dzwò-yi-dzwə. (B) Wǒ shìr gǔng-rən. (C) Měi-yǒu
chyán.

12. Dzài-djyàn.
(A) Mǎi-mai-rən. (B) Dzài-djyàn. (C) Bu-yàu.

EIGHTH SESSION

CLINCHING THEM

DO THIS: Spend about 10 minutes on the tone exercises of
the Fifth Session. Then use the cover-up memory method
(see page 21) on the sentences of the Sixth Session.

PRACTICAL TEST

Use the Practical Dictionary but don't look up more than one word for each problem.

1. You see a girl at a dance. You think she is the kid sister of your friend Li in Peiping. Say *Excuse me.*

2. Ask her if she is Miss Li.

3. Ask her if she's from Peiping.

4. Ask how her brother is.

5. She answers, **Tă hău.** What does that mean?

6. Tell her you're glad.

7. Introduce her to your friend by saying, *This is my friend, Jack Jones.*

8. Introduce her to Jack's father by saying, *This is Mr. Jones, my friend's father.*

9. Ask Miss Li if she'd care to dance.

10. Ask if she likes the music.

11. Later you go to a tea room. Ask Miss Li what she'll have.

12. Can you say *Good night* without looking up any words?

Expressions built with the word for "Person"

ON THE SOUNDS, FINAL

SHARPENING UP

The main requirement in your pronunciation of Chinese is that you get the right sound in each word, so that people can make out what you are saying. This you have learned from your study of the First Session. However, it is worth your while to review now so as to be sure you have it all straight.

DO THIS: Go thru the First Session again, concentrating on any point you are not sure of. Also review the Fifth Session, on tones.

Beyond speaking understandably, you may want to polish up your pronunciation so it doesn't sound like a heavy foreign accent to the Chinese. This Session discusses and gives practical exercises on sounds that English-speaking people are most likely to pronounce in un-Chinese fashion. However, to make real progress in this, you definitely need the help of a Chinese speaker. If there is none available to you right now, skip this Session.

1. Get your Chinese speaker to pronounce the words:

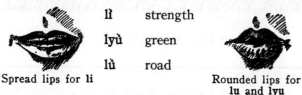

lǐ	strength
lyǜ	green
lù	road

Spread lips for li

Rounded lips for
lu and lyu

Notice that *green* sounds more like *strength* than like *road*. But, if you watch your Chinese speaker as he says the words, you will see that he puckers up his lips for *green* in about the same way as for *road*. In other words, **lyǜ** is pronounced like **lǐ** but with the lips rounded; this is the sound that corresponds to **u** in the Romanization every time it follows **y** except in the combination **yung**, which has the normal value for **u**. Here are some words for practice:

> **chǐ yì nǐ yǎn** (gas, idea, you, eye)
> **chyù yù nyǔ yuǎn** (go, jail, female, far)

2. Ask your Chinese speaker to say:

sìr	four
sə̀	color

Teeth together
in saying sir

Mouth slightly open
in saying sə

Both words are a little like English *sir*. **Sìr** has the teeth close together and the tongue held high in the mouth; there is something of a buzzing sound to it. **Sə̀** is said with the mouth partly open, the tongue relaxed; like *sub* minus the *b*. Study the sound both by listening and by watching your speaker's mouth. The vowel sound **ir** comes only after *s-* and *sh-* type consonants; we give words with **ə** for comparison:

sìr tsìr dzìr shìr chìr djìr (four, stab, word-sign, be, eat, paper)

sə̀ tsə̀ dzə́ shə̀ chə̀ djə̀ (color, toilet, duty, shoot, wagon, this)

3. Have your Chinese speaker pronounce these sets of words:

sǎu sǎn tsǎu dzù (sweep, three, grass, rent)
shǎu shǎn chǎu djù (few, mountain, fry, live)
shyǎu shyǎn chyǎu djyə̌u (small, first, shallow, then)

In many parts of central, southern, and western China, the second set of words is pronounced exactly like the first. In the regions that use **sh ch dj**, the Chinese sounds are different from the English, being made with the tongue curled back in the mouth; often it seems as tho they are putting an *r* into the syllable, making our example seem like *srau, sran, tsrau, dzru*. You must try to imitate your Chinese speaker. If you pronounce an ordinary English *sh*, *ch* and *dj*, it may sound to your Chinese friends as tho you were saying words of the third set.

COMPARATIVE TONGUE POSITIONS

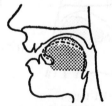

In Pronouncing
Chinese **chau**

In Chinese **chyau**
(same as for **yau**)

English **ch** shown by dotted lines

The third set of words shows combinations with the **y**-sound; the first sounds are modified so they sound in between

English *s*, *ts*, *dz* and English *sh*, *ch*, *dj*. The same modification takes place when *sh* etc. come before *i* (but not the sound which we spell *ir*). Examples:

shì shìn chì chìn-chìn djì djìn   (west, new, seven, kiss, chicken, enter)

4. Have your Chinese speaker say:

ròu rén rúng-yi ràng   (meat, person, easy, allow)

Some Chinese use a *y*-sound instead of an *r* in these words. The Chinese *r*-sound is made with a rub, so that it slightly resembles the middle sound in *seizure, azure, measure, treasure*, etc. However, it is made with the tongue curled back in the mouth—just like Chinese *sh* etc. as described under 3. If you happen to know Czech, Polish, or Russian, make this sound like the one shown by *ř*, *rz* and *ж* in the alphabets of these languages.

5. Have your speaker pronounce:

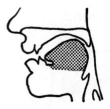

**hǒ hǎu hwǎ
hǒn húng**

(river, good, words,
very, red)

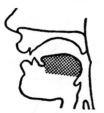

Raised tongue
causing scrape in
Chinese **hau**

Low tongue sound
without scrape
in English *how*

There is a scrape to the *h*-sound in Chinese, like what is shown by *j* in Spanish, *x* in Russian and Greek, *ch* in Dutch. You can get the sound by mimicking your Chinese speaker.

6. Listen carefully as your speaker says the following:

pàu twǝi tsài chū kǎu   (cannon, push, vegetables, out, bake)
bàu dwǝi dzài djū gǎu   (report, pile, again, pig, pick-ax)

You may be able to detect the slight difference between each of these sounds and the corresponding English one. Chinese **p t ts ch k** are generally pronounced with much more breath force than the English sounds. Chinese **b d dz dj g** are characterized by having a bit more pressure of the lips or tongue than we have, and the vocal cords do not vibrate. It may occasionally seem as tho you are hearing **p t** etc., but don't let this fool you into changing the sounds. If you get the fine points of Chinese pronunciation, it must not be at the cost of confusing the essentials.

DO THIS: Practice all the examples given under each point above.

DICTATION

Let your Chinese speaker dictate words taken at random from the examples. Write them out and later check your spelling with what is given above.

TALKING UNIT THREE
COUNTING AND ARITHMETIC

TENTH SESSION
FIGURES

One, two, three, four	Yì èr sān sìr
Five, six, seven, eight	Wǔ lyòu chī bā
Nine, ten, eleven, twelve	Djyǒu shír shír-yì shír-èr
Twenty, thirty, forty, fifty	èr-shir sān-shr sìr-shir wǔ-shir
Sixty, seventy, eighty, ninety	Lyòu-shir chī-shir bā-shir djyǒu-shir
One-hundred, one-thousand one-tenthousand	Yì-bǎi yì-chyǎn yí-wǎn
100-tenthousand (1,000,000)	Yì-bai-wǎn
One-thousand, nine-hundred, zero, nine (1909)	Yì-chyǎn, djyóu-bǎi, líng, djyǒu
Three add-three be-six (3 + 3 = 6)	Sān djyǎ-sān shìr-lyòu
Four subtract-one be-three (4 − 1 = 3)	Sìr djyǎn-yì shìr-sān
Correct-not-correct	Dwèi-bu-dwèi
Correct	Dwèi-lə
Not-correct	Bú-dwèi
Howmany-item person (How many people?)	Djǐ-gə rén

42

Haven't (There aren't any)	**Méi-yǒu**
One-item person (One person)	**Yí-gə rén**
Two-item person (Two people)	**Lyǎng-gə rén**
Two-lump-money (Two dollars)	**Lyǎng-kwài chyán**
One-item clock (One clock)	**Yí-gə djüng**
One-mark-clock (One o'clock)	**Yì-dyǎn-djüng**
One-item clock-head (One hour)	**Yí-gə djüng-tóu**
Five-division-money (Five cents)	**Wǔ-fən-chyán**
Five-division-clock (Five minutes)	**Wǔ-fən-djüng**
Five-mark fifty-division (5:50)	**Wú-dyǎn wǔ-shir-fən**
Howmany kilometer	**Dwə-shǎu güng-lǐ**
Five English-mile be eight-kilometer	**Wǔ-Ying-lǐ shìr bā-güng-lǐ**
One-year	**Yì-nyán**
One-ageyear (One year old)	**Yí-swèi**

Explanations

Point 21. The numbers from 11 to 19 are made by combining ten with 1, 2, 3 etc. That is, it is like saying *ten and one, ten and two* and so forth.

Counting from 20 to 90 by tens, you do just the opposite, saying *two-tens, three-tens* and so on. Twenty-one is *two-ten-one.*

Point 22. The Chinese have a special word for *ten-thousand* (**wàn**) and the higher numbers are built up with this word.

Point 23. The word **líng** means *zero.* In giving big num-bers you put in the word *zero* in cases like:

1,001 (one-thousand, zero, one) **Yi-chyǎn líng yǐ**
10,050 (one-tenthousand, zero, **Yi-wǎn líng wǔ-shir**
  fifty)

If you hear someone say **yǐ-bǎi-ər**, that is short for **yǐ-bǎi-ər-shir**, meaning 120 and not 102. In the same way **yǐ-chyǎn-wǔ** (one-thousand-five) is short for 1,500.

COUNTING

Do each exercise over and over till it comes easily.

1. Count from one to 10 and backwards from 10 to one.
2. To 20 and back by twos.
3. To 30 and back by threes.
4. To 40 and back by fours.
5. To 50 and back by fives.
6. To 100 and back by tens.
7. To 110 and back by elevens.
8. To 120 and back by twelves.
9. To 1000 by hundreds.
10. To 10,000 by thousands.
11. To 100,000 by tenthousands.
12. Read the following numbers out loud:

18	119	2002	30,003	12,345
41	190	2020	33,300	54,321
72	109	2200	30,300	93,713

ELEVENTH SESSION
HOW THEY'RE BUILT

DO THIS: Spend about 10 minutes practicing the sounds in the Ninth Session. Then go thru the expressions given in the Tenth.

Explanations

Point 24. The expression for *nothing* is different from the word for *zero.* You say *It isn't what* (**Bú-shìr shə́m-mə**) for *It's nothing. There aren't any* is **mə́i-yŏu** (haven't).

Point 25. When you count things in Chinese, you have to throw in a word, called a classifier, which describes the thing in a general way, something like what we do in English when we say, *one head of cattle, one stick of wood, one round of ammunition.* In Chinese, it goes much farther and you say, for example: one-stem pencil, one-sheet map, one-structure house, one-strip road, and so forth. You can find the more important classifiers in the Practical Dictionary under the word *one,* but better not bother about them. For now, you can get along very well by always using the syllable **gə,** the same as in **djə̀-gə** (this) and **nà-gə** (that). This is the right classifier for words referring to people, most animals and all objects not otherwise classified. Furthermore, the Chinese themselves often use it in place of other syllables.

Try to get into the habit of using **gə** whenever you speak of a given number of anything, for example:

Here have howmany-item person (How many people are there here?)	**Djə̀-li yə́u djǐ-gə rə́n**
Have three-item (There are three)	**Yŏu sān-gə**

Point 26. The numbers can also be combined with measure-words, that is, words that give units of amount, like: one-package, one-pair, one-lump, one-liter, one-kilometer, one-day, one-year and so forth. A few of the measure words are given in the Tenth Session. Find the others in the Practical Dictionary when you need them.

Note that one-lump (**yǐ-kwǎi**) is used for loaves of bread, cakes of soap, dollars of money etc.

Also note that a year of age is expressed differently from a year's length of time.

How many years?—Five years   **Djǐ-nyán—Wǔ-nyán**
How old?—Five years old   **Djǐ-swǎi—Wǔ-swǎi**

Point 27. For weights and measures, the Chinese use many different systems. The easiest of them is the metric system, the same as that used in many other parts of the world. In case you don't know: 100 centimeters = 1 meter, 1000 meters = 1 kilometer; 1000 grams = 1 kilogram, 1000 kilograms = 1 metric ton, which is 2200 pounds. A liter is a little more than an American quart. For length, 5 centimeters = 2 inches, 9 meters = 10 yards, 8 kilometers = 5 mi.

You will find the metric units in the Practical Dictionary. All of them begin with the word **gūng** meaning *public* or *universal*. When the Chinese speak of our units they use **Yǐng** for *English*.

Point 28. **Fǝn,** meaning *division*, is used for various small units of measure. In the metric system, **gūng-fǝn** is either a gram or a centimeter. And **fǝn** is also used for money and time:

Five-division-money (five cents)   **wǔ-fǝn-chyán**
Five-division-clock (five minutes) **wǔ-fǝn-djǔng**

Point 29. Numbers used with **djǔng**, meaning *bell* or *clock*, can express the number of clocks or of hours or the time of day:

one-item clock (one clock)   **yǐ-gǝ djǔng**
one-item clock-head (one hour)   **yǐ-gǝ djǔng-tóu**
one-mark-clock (one o'clock)   **yǐ-dyǎn-djǔng**

To give time in hours and minutes, the expression can be shortened:

five-mark fifty-five (5:55) **wú-dyǎn wǔ-shir-wǔ**

Point 30. There are two words for *two*: **ə̀r** is used in saying the number by itself and in making higher numbers. **Lyǎng** is used with classifiers and measure-words, when speaking of just two, but not for 22 or 200 and so forth.

one, two, three, four **yî ə̀r sān sìr**
two-hundred-twenty-two **ə̀r-bǎi-ə̀r-shir-ə̀r**
two people **lyǎng-gə rə́n**
twenty-two people **ə̀r-shir-ə̀r-gə rə́n**
two o'clock **lyǎng-dyǎn-djüng**
twelve o'clock **shír-ə̀r-dyǎn-djüng**

However, getting the two words mixed up will not prevent people from understanding you.

Point 31. The word **djǐ** means either *a few, several* or *how many?* In speaking of large numbers, **dwə̄-shǎu** (much-little) is used. For example, **dwə̄-shǎu** is usual in talking about money, **djǐ** in speaking of a person's age:

How much money? **Dwə̄-shǎu-chyán**
How old are you? **Ní djǐ-swə̀i**

PRACTICAL TEST

1. Count out loud the people in each of these groups, saying: **yí-gə rə́n, lyǎng-gə rən, sān-gə rən,** etc.

(A)   (B)   (C)

2. (A) Count everybody in problem one. (B) Count all the men. (C) All the women.

3. Count the clocks in each group, saying; **yí-gə djūng, lyǎng-gə djūng**, etc.

(A)   (B)

(C)

4. (A) Count all clocks in problem three. (B) All alarm clocks. (C) All mantel clocks.

5. Tell the time on each clock:

6. Answer the following questions about yourself: (A) **Ní djǐ-swèi.** (B) **Yǒu djǐ-gə hái-dz.** (C) **Nǐ-də fù-chin djǐ-swèi.** (D) **Nǐ-də mǔ-chin djǐ-swèi.**

7. (A) Name the present year. (B) What was it twelve years ago? (C) 140 years ago? (D) What will it be 100 years from now?

8. Read out loud and give in Chinese the solutions to the following problems:

(A) **Yí-gə djūng shǐr wǔ-kwài-chyán. Wǔ-gə djūng shǐr dwē-shǎu chyán.**

(B) **Yí-gə gūng-rən yǎu chī-kwài-chyán. Sān-gə rən yǎu dwē-shǎu chyán.**

(C) **Wē-yǒu sǐr-kwài-chyán, ní yǒu sān-kwài, tā yǒu shír-kwài. Wē-mən yǒu dwē-shǎu chyán.**

TWELFTH SESSION
CLINCHING THEM

DO THIS: Spend about 10 minutes on the tone exercises of the Fifth Session. When you count or do simple arithmetic problems, try not to get into a sing-song and forget about the proper tones of the words. Keep your tones correct all the time.

Use the cover-up method on the expressions of the Tenth Session.

PRACTICAL TEST

1. Read off the following addition problems, giving the answer along with the problem, like this:

Problem: 3   +   3   =
You say: **sān djyā-sān shìr-lyòu**

(A) 1+0=   (B) 1+1=   (C) 1+2=   (D) 1+3=
(E) 1+4=   (F) 1+5=   (G) 1+6=   (H) 1+7=
(I) 1+8=   (J) 1+9=   (K) 2+2=   (L) 4+4=
(M) 5+5=   (N) 2+5=   (O) 3+4=   (P) 5+2=
(Q) 4+5=   (R) 3+3=

2. Read off these subtraction problems:

Example: 3   −   3   =
You say: **sān djyǎn-sān shìr-líng.**

(A) 10−2=   (B) 10−3=   (C) 10−4=   (D) 10−5=
(E) 10−6=   (F) 9−7=   (G) 4−3=   (H) 2−1=
(I) 7−3=   (J) 9−3=   (K) 9−4=   (L) 6−2=

3. Using the Practical Dictionary when necessary, ask and answer the following questions:

(A) How many brothers have you?
(B) How many sisters have you?
(C) How many friends have you in St. Louis?
(D) How many people are there here?
(E) One cup of coffee is fifty dollars. How much is ten cups?

TALKING UNIT FOUR
ON DIFFERENT TOPICS

THIRTEENTH SESSION
TALKING BUSINESS

You know-not-know (Do you know?)	Nǐ djǐr-dǎu bu-djǐr-dǎu
Wang-Mr. located-what-place (Where's Mr. Wang?)	Wáng-Shyan-shəng dzài shə́m-mə dǐ-fang
He reach-store-in go-done (He's gone to the store)	Tā dǎu-pù-dz-li chyù-lə
Buy things (to buy things)	mǎi dūng-shi
Eh? or Huh? (What did you say?)	Á
Face-not-up (I'm in the wrong, I'm sorry)	Dwə̀i-bu-chǐ
Invite again-speak one-time (Please repeat)	Chǐng dzài-shwə̄ yí-tsìr
I not-be China-person	Wə̌ bú-shìr Djūng-gwə-rən
I not-understand	Wə̌ bù-dǔng
Not-knowhow speak China-words	Bú-hwə̀i shwə̄ Djūng-gwə-hwà
I-understand-belonging very little (My understanding is very little)	Wə̌-dǔng-də hə́n-shǎu
Don't speak-belonging too-fast (Don't speak too fast)	Byə̀ shwə̄-də tài-kwài

51

Wang-Mr. what-time return-come (When'll Mr. Wang come back?)	Wáng-Shyan-shəng shə́m-mə shír-həu hwə́i-lai
Howmany-mark clock (What o'clock?)	Djí-dyăn-djŭng
Return-come-belonging time (When he comes back)	Hwə́i-lai-də shír-həu
Invite-tell-him (please ask him)	Chĭng-djyău-ta
Give-me take-this-pants patch-one-patch (to mend these pants for me)	gə́i-wə̆ bă-djə̀-gə-kù-dz bŭ-yi-bu
Pickup-him go (Take them)	Ná-ta chyu
Put located-there (Put them there)	Fàng dzài-nă-li
Much-thanks	Dwə̆-shyə̀

Explanations

Point 32. Many words, of the kind called nouns, end in **dz** when they stand alone, but drop this ending when they are used in combinations with other words. Examples:

store, book-store	pù-dz, shŭ-pù
knife, stab-knife (bayonet)	dău-dz, tsìr-dău

On the same principle, a great many two-syllable words in Chinese are simplified to one syllable when used in combinations. Examples:

machine, fly-machine (airplane)	djī-chĭ, fə̆i-djī
peace, North-peace (city of Peiping)	hə́-píng, Bə̆i-ping
thanks, many thanks	shyə̀-shyə, dwə̆-shyə̀

Point 33. The word **hǒn** can sometimes be translated as *very*, but in other cases it seems to be used to round an expression out into two syllables. In these cases, it is better to think of **hǒn** as meaning *rather.*

He speak-belonging rather-fast (He speaks fast)	**Tā-shwǒ-də hǒn-kwài**
We person rather-much (We are many people. There are a lot of us)	**Wǒ-mən rǒn hǒn-dwǒ**

Point 34. Notice the way you put your words together to say *he talks fast.* Follow the same model in saying things like:

He-do-belonging good (He does well)	**Tā-dzwǒ-də hǎu**
I Chinese-language speak-belonging not-good (I don't speak Chinese well)	**Wǒ Djūng-wǒn shwǒ-də bu-hǎu**

Point 35. Our word *know* translates several different Chinese words. These include **hwài** for knowing how to do a thing and **djir-dàu** for knowing a fact or an object.

Me knowhow-do (I know how to do it)	**Wǒ hwài-dzwǒ**
Me not-know that word	**Wǒ bù-djir-dàu nà-gə hwà**

In the Practical Dictionary you will find still another word for *know, be acquainted with a person.* Whenever you look up a word, you must notice the different Chinese equivalents and decide from the explanations and examples which one fits your meaning.

Point 36. Our advice to you has been never to translate word-for-word from English. This is particularly true of words like *to*. If you look in the Dictionary, you will find three different equivalents. In cases like *he wants to go, he came to see me, it is good to eat*, you simply forget about it. For going to, you use **dàu** meaning *reach*. For sending or selling or handing a thing to a person, you use the word for *give*. Example:

He reach-Peiping come sell-thing give-me (He comes to Peiping to sell things to me)	**Tā dàu-Běi-píng lái mǎi-dūng-shi gěi-wǒ**

Point 37. **Gěi**, meaning *give*, is also the most usual equivalent of *for* when you speak of doing something for someone. In this use, the **gěi** comes ahead of the main verb.

He give-me do-job (He works for me)	**Tā gěi-wǒ dzwò-shìr**

Point 38. In the First Session you learned to use *Is it O.K.?* in asking a favor; now you get the regular word for *please*, which is the same as *invite*.

Invite-come (Please come)	**Chǐng-lái**
Invite-you come (same meaning)	**Chǐng-nǐ lái**
I-invite-him come (I invite him to come)	**Wǒ-chǐng-tā lái**

Point 39. The ideas of bringing and taking in Chinese are broken into two parts, handling the thing and going or coming.

Lead-me go (Take me along)	**Dài-wǒ chyu**
Lead-him come (Bring him along)	**Dài-ta lái**

| Pickup-come (Bring it) | **Ná-lai** |
| Pickup-clock go (Take the clock) | **Ná-djŭng chyu** |

Similarly, various kinds of action on specifically indicated objects are expressed with the help of the word **bǎ**, which means *take hold*, as in these examples:

Take-that patch-one-patch (Mend that)	**Bǎ-nǎ-gə bŭ-yi-bu**
Take-this look-one-look (Look this over)	**Bǎ-djǎ-gə kǎn-yi-kan**
Take-clock buy (Buy the clock)	**Bǎ-djŭng mǎi**

Point 40. The word for telling a person to do something is **djyàu** and sounds exactly like the word for *call* or *called*.

| This called pants | **Djǎ-gə djyàu kù-dz** |
| Tell-him come | **Djyàu-ta lái** |

Point 41. **Hwéi,** meaning *return*, sounds like **hwǎi,** meaning *know how*, except for the tone. Here's a sentence to practice on:

| I not-knowhow return-go (I don't know how to go back) | **Wǒ bú-hwǎi hwéi-chyu** |

PRACTICAL TEST

Solve by looking for any words you need among the expressions at the beginning of this Session.

1. You meet a friend. Ask where he's going.
2. He says: **Dàu-pù-dz-li.** What does this mean?
3. Ask him what he intends to buy.

4. He answers: **Hǒn-dwǒ dūng-shi.** What does this mean?
5. Supposing you don't understand, how do you say so?
6. If your friend talks too fast, what do you say?
7. How do you ask him to repeat?
8. Ask your friend if it is a good store.
9. Ask him if they have clocks.
10. Ask him to please buy a clock for you.
11. He says: **Wǒ gǒi dwǒ-shǎu chyán.** What does that mean? Give him an answer.
12. Your friend asks what time it is. Tell him you don't know.
13. Say: *When you buy the clock, I'll know what time it is.*
14. Your friend says: **Hǒn-hǎu. Dzǎi-djyǎn.** What is the meaning? Tell him: *Many thanks.*

FOURTEENTH SESSION
GENERAL REVIEW

DO THIS: Run thru the sentences in the Thirteenth Session with your Chinese speaker. Then use the cover-up method on them.

To Help You Understand

Some expressions given in the Thirteenth Session can be helpful when you are trying to understand people speaking. You can say: *Eh? I'm sorry, Please repeat, I don't understand, I understand very little, Don't speak too fast.* Learn these phrases by heart.

PRACTICAL TEST

Pick out the right replies.
1. **Nǐ dzwǒ shǒm-mə shǐr.**

(A) Dzwə̀ kù-dz. (B) Dzwə̀ dzə̀i-pù-dz-li. (C) Gə̆i-tə̀i-tai chyán.

2. Nǐ hwə̀i-bu-hwə̀i bǔ wə̆-də kù-dz.

(A) Hwə̀i-shwə̄ Djüng-gwə-hwə̀. (B) Bu-djir-də̀u. (C) Djə̀-gə djyə̀u shə́m-mə.

3. Chǐng kàn-yi-kan.

(A) Hǎu. (B) Də̀u-pù-dz-li chyu. (C) Wə̆ shìr Lǐ-Tai-tai.

4. Nǐ yə̆u-məi-yə̆u shír-həu bǔ djə̀-gə.

(A) Wǔ-gə rə́n. (B) Dwə̄-shǎu-dūng-shi. (C) Yə̆u.

5. Wə́ djí-dyǎn-djüng hwə́i-lai.

(A) Wú-dyǎn-djüng. (B) Wə̆ bu-dzwə̀ shə́m-mə. (C) Mə́i-yə̆u djüng.

6. Dwə̄-shǎu chyán.

(A) Hə̆n-dwə̄ bing. (B) Dwə̄-shyə̀. (C) Yí-kwə̀i Mə̆i-gwə-chyán.

7. Chǐng dzə̀i-shwə̄ yí-tsìr.

(A) Mə́i-yə̆u shír-həu. (B) Mǎi-mai-rən. (C) Yí-kwə̀i Mə̆i-gwə-chyán.

REVIEW TEST

Give the Chinese for the following words. Perfect score 120. If you miss more than 30, better do some reviewing.

1. China, America, person, child, wife, husband, mother, father, teacher, workman.

2. Mr., Mrs., merchant, soldier, I, you, he, she, it, we.

3. They, them, you-folks, him, her, here, there, where, what, when.

4. Still, again, how much, what o'clock, how many years, how old, five dollars, five minutes, five cents, five kilometers.

5. Zero, 1, 2, 3, 4, 5, 6, 7, 8, 9.

6. 10, 20, 30, 40, 50, 60, 70, 80, 90, 100.

7. 1000, 10,000, add, subtract, money, store, pants, clock, thing, time.

8. Buy, sell, come, go, do, make, work, sit, look, want.

9. Give, take, bring, understand, know, know how, tell to do, repair, return, invite.

10. Bring, take, take along, pick up, put, located, reach, good, bad, fast.

11. Much, little, correct, fairly, very, too, is, am, are, be.

12. His, yours, he's come, how about that? excuse me, it's so, it isn't so, hello, good-by, thanks.

FIFTEENTH SESSION
CHOOSE YOUR OWN SUBJECT

In using the Practical Dictionary, remember it has only some of the most common words. If you don't find a word, think of another way of saying the same thing or of describing it.

If you expect to talk a lot about certain special things that aren't to be found in this Dictionary, make a list of the words on the blank pages at the end. Be practical rather than ambitious in making your list. Remember that long lists are hard to use. You can get the words for your special list from an interpreter or a large dictionary or by pointing at things and asking Chinese people: **Djà-gə djyàu shə́m-mə.**

Unless you are in an awful hurry, when you look up a word in the Practical Dictionary, take a moment to study the various details that are given about the word: other English meanings of the same word, the meaning of the parts of compound forms, examples showing how to use the expression, other Chinese words that sound alike and may cause confusion. This additional information helps you to use the word correctly and to remember it more easily.

Suggestions for the Typewriter: If you expect to be typing out things in Romanized Chinese, you can use plain *e* instead of ə. If you want to include tone-signs, you can have a set of accent marks (⁻ ´ ˇ ˋ) installed on your machine, to be used in place of the arrows. A French typewriter has ´ and ˋ and these can be combined into ˇ; for the level tone a hyphen can be used by turning the roller slightly to space it higher.

PRACTICAL TEST

Using the Practical Dictionary, carry on a conversation on any topic, such as those suggested below. You can do it as make-believe with your Chinese speaker or, better yet, in a real situation. It is a good idea to prepare for this test by thinking in advance of some of the things you'll want to say and making a list of words you will need.

1. An invitation to a Chinese home. Conversation about family and friends, interests, work, food.

2. Take something to a shop to be repaired or cleaned. Explain what is to be done, ask the cost and when it will be ready.

3. A little shopping trip.

4. Interview a man you want to hire. Ask what he can do, where he worked before, etc. Arrange about salary and explain duties.

5. Demonstrate and explain how to start and drive a car, or how to handle some other piece of machinery.

6. Ask information from a local farmer about how to get to a given place, condition of the road, etc.

HAU-BU-HAU

Knowing the Chinese words **hau** (good) and **bu-hau** (not-good) is a big help. This little story can be understood after learning the Seventeen Sentences of the Second Session.

A

a **yí-gə** (*same as* one, *but commonly omitted*; *also see other forms listed under* one)

ability, skill **gūng-fu** (*also* spare time)

able to **nə́ng**: I'm able to do it **wə̌ nə́ng-dzwə̀** (I able-do)

about, concerning **dàu** (*same as* reach): they talk about him **tā-mən shwə̄-dàu-ta** (they speak-reach-him), think about that **shyǎng dàu-nà-gə** (think reach-that)

about, more or less **chà-bu-dwə̄** (difference-not-much): about thirty **chà-bu-dwə̄ sān-shir-gə**

above, on **shàng** (*same as* up) *or* **shàng-byan** (up-side): above the mountain **dzài-shān shàng-byan** (located-mountain up-side)

accelerator, throttle **chì-mə̌n** (gas-door)

account **djàng**

accountant **gwǎn-djàng-də** (manage-account-belonging)

acid **swān** (*also* sour): hydrochloric acid **yán-swān** (salt-acid), sulfuric acid **lyə́u-swān** (sulfur-acid)

across **hə́ng** (*same as* crosswise) *or* **gwə̀** (*same as* to cross): there's a stick across the road **yə̌u gùn-dz hə́ng dzài-lù-shang** (have stick across located-road-on), he goes across the road **tā dzə̌u gwə̀-lù chyu** (he walk across-road go)

act, perform **yǎn-shí** (perform-drama)

act, pretend to be **djyǎ-djwǎng**

actor **shì-dz** *or* **yǎn-yuán** (perform-personnel)

add up **djyā-chi-lai** (add-up-come): add it up **bǎ-ta djyā-chi-lai** (take-it add-up-come) adjust **tyáu-djǒng**

adult **dà-rən** (big-person)

advance **chyán-djìn** (front-enter)

advertise **dǝng-gwǎng-gàu** (mount-broad-inform)

advertisement **gwǎng-gàu**

advice, suggestion **djú-yi**

advise **chū-djú-yi** (out-suggestion)

afraid, afraid of **pà**: I'm afraid of it **wǒ pà-ta** (I afraid-it)

after **yǐ-hòu**: he left after I came **wǒ-lái-lə yǐ-hòu tā djyòu dzǒu-lə** (I-come-done after, he then leave-done)

afternoon **shyà-wǔ** (down-noon): I'll go in the afternoon **wǒ shyà-wǔ chyù** (I afternoon go)

afterwards **hòu-lái** (behind-come)

again **yòu** (*referring to the past*) *or* **dzài** (*referring to future*): he came again **tā yòu lái-lə** (he again come-done), say it again **dzài-shwō** (again-speak)

again and again **yí-tsìr yòu yi-tsir** (once again once)

against, not in favor **bú-dzàn-chéng** (not-agree)

age **swèi** (*meaning* years old): what's his age **tā djǐ-swèi** (he howmany-years), thirty years of age **sān-shir-swèi** (three-ten-years)

agent, representative **dài-byǎu** (substitute-represent)

agency, branch office **fēn-háng** (division-firm)

ago **yǐ-chyán** (*same as* before): one month ago **yí-gə yuè yǐ-chyán** (one-item month before)

agree **túng-yì** (same-mind): I agree with you **wǒ gēn-nǐ túng-yì** (I with-you same-mind)

ahead, first **shyǎn**: go on ahead **nǐ shyǎn-dzǒu** (you first-walk)

aim, take aim **myǎu-djǔn** (sight-accurate)

air **kūng-chì** (air-gas): air force **kūng-djyūn** (air-army), air raid **kūng-shí**

airfield **fēi-djī-chǎng** (airplane-field)

airplane **fēi-dji** (fly-machine)

alarm **djǐng-bàu** (warning-report)

alcohol **djyǒu-djǐng** (wine-essence)

alive, living **hwó-dj** (live-remain): he's still alive **tā hái hwó-dj** or **tā hái-dzài** (he still-located)

all **dōu** (*also* both): all of you come **nǐ-mən dōu-lái** (youfolks all-come)

all clear! **djyǒ-chú** (loosen-remove)

allied country **túng-méng-gwó** (same-oath-country)

allow, let **djǔn**: let him go **djǔn-ta chyù**

allowed, permissible **kǒ-yi**: smoking isn't allowed here **djò-li bù-kǒ-yi chōu-yān** (here not-allowed suck-tobacco), I'm not allowed to go **wǒ bù-kǒ-yi chyù** (I now-allowed go)

almost, more or less **chà-bu-dwō** (difference-not-much)

alone **yí-gə-rən** (one-person): I live alone **wǒ yí-gə-rən djù** (I one-person live)

along, alongside **shùn-dj**: along the river **shùn-dj hó**

aloud **dà-shōng** (big-sound): he spoke aloud **tā dà-shōng shwō-hwà** (he big-sound speak-word)

alphabet **dzìr-mǔ** (word-mother)

already **yǐ-djǐng** (finish-pass): he has already come **tā yǐ-djǐng lái-lə** (he already come-done)

also **yǒ** (*sounds like* wild): he also comes **tā yǒ-lái**

always **yúng-yuǎn** (ever-far): he has always lived here **tā yúng-yuǎn djù dzài-djò-li** (he always live located-here)

am, is, are **shìr** (*more information under* be)

ambassador **dà-shìr** (big-courier)

ambulance **djyòu-hù-chō** (save-nursing-vehicle)

ambush, to ambush **mái-fu** (bury-ambush)

America, United States **Mǒi-gwə**: American **Mǒi-gwə-də** (America-belonging); an American **Mǒi-gwə-rón** (America-person)

ammunition **dàn-yàu** (shall-medicine)

amount **shù-mu** (number-index); large amount **hǒn-dwē**
(very-much); small amount **hán-shǎu** (very-little)

ampere **ǎn-pέi** (like English): five amperes **wǔ-ǎn-pέi**

amplifier, loud speaker **fàng-dà-chǐ** (let-big-device)

and **gēn** (*same as* with): you and I **wǒ gēn-nǐ** (I with-you)

anesthetic **má-yàu** (numb-medicine)

angle, corner **djyǎu** (*sounds like* foot): right angle **djír-
djyǎu** (straight-angle)

angry **shēng-chǐ-lǝ** (born-steam-done)

angular measure **djyǎu-dù** (angle-degree)

animal **dùng-wu** (move-thing)

Annam, Indo-China **Ǎn-nán** (safe-south)

annoy **má-fan**

answer **hwέi-dá** (return-answer)

antenna **tyǎn-shyàn** (sky-wire)

any (*omitted in questions*): are there any people here? **djɘ̀-li
yǒu-mɘi-yǒu rέn** (here have-haven't person)

any at all **swέi-byàn** (according-convenience): anyone at
all can come **swέi-byàn nǎ-yí-gɘ rέn dōu kέ-yi lái** (according-convenience which person all allowed come)

apple **píng-gwǒ** (apple-fruit)

approximately **chà-bu-dwō** (difference-not-much)

are, is, am, be **shǐr** (*more information under* be)

arm **gɘ̄-bɘi**

armature **dyàn-shū** (electric-core)

armored forces **djwǎng-djyǎ bù-dwèi** (install-shell section-
team)

arms, fire-arms **chyāng-pàu** (gun-cannon)

army **lù-djyūn** (mainland-army)

around **rǎu-dj**: he goes around the tree **tā rǎu-dj shù dzǒu**
(he around tree walk)

arrange (put things in order) **djéng-lǐ**

arrange for, make arrangements **chέu-bèi** (plan-prepare)

arrest **djwə-chi-lai** (arrest-up-come): arrest him **bǎ-tā djwə-chi-lai** (take-him arrest)

arrive, reach **dǎu**

artillery, artilleryman **pǎu-bǐng** (cannon-soldier)

artillery piece **pǎu**

as, equally **yí-yàng** (one-manner): you're as good as I **nǐ gēn-wǒ yí-yàng hǎu** (you with-me one-manner good)

ashamed **tsán-kwəi**

ashes **hwəi**

Asia **Yà-djəu** (Ya-continent)

ask for, beg **yǎu** (*also* want): go ask for food **chyù yǎu-fàn** (go ask-food), he asks me for money **tā wən-wǒ yǎu-chyán** (he inquire-me ask-money)

ask, inquire **wən**: he asks if it's so **tā wən shìr-bu-shìr** (he inquire be-not-be)

asleep **shwəi-djáu-lə** (sleep-attain-done)

assemble, get together **djyù-hwəi** (assemble-meet)

assemble, put together (machine parts) **pəi-hə́** (mate-together): assemble that machine **bǎ-nà-gə dji-chì pəi-hə́-chi-lai** (take-that machine assemble-up-come)

assorted, mixed **shír-djìn-də** (ten-variety-belonging)

at, located at **dzài**: he's at that place **tā dzài-nà-gə-dì-fang** (him located-that-place)

Atlantic Ocean **Dà-shi-yang** (Big-west-ocean)

attack **gūng-dji** (offensive-strike)

Australia **Àu-djeu** (Au-continent)

automatic **dzìr-dùng-də** (self-move-belonging)

automobile **chì-chə́** (gas-vehicle)

autumn **chyə̌u-tyan**

awake **shǐng-lə** (awake-done): is he awake? **tā shǐng-lə mə́i-yǒu** (he wake-done haven't)

ax **fǔ-dz**

axle, pivot, axis **djə́u**

B

back (of person or animal) **bèi**

back of, behind **hòu-byan** (rear-side): backdoor **hòu-mén** (rear-door)

back again, to return **hwéi**: come back **hwéi-lai** (return-come)

bad, no good **bù-hǎu** (not-good)

bad, in bad shape, spoiled **hwài-lə**

badge, insignia **hwěi-djǎng**

bag, sack **kǒu-dài** (mouth-bag): one bagful **yí-dài**, three bags of rice **sān-dài mǐ** (three-bag rice)

baggage **shíng-li**

bake **kǎu**

bakelite, plastic **djyǎu-mù** (glue-wood)

balance remaining **djyé-tswén** (conclude-remain)

balanced account **djyé-djàng** (conclude-account)

ball **chyóu**: to play ball **dǎ-chyóu** (hit-ball)

bamboo **djú-dz**

banana **shyǎng-djyāu**

band, strap **dài-dz** (*sounds like* bag)

band, orchestra **yuè-dwèi** (music-team)

bandage **bēng-dài** (taut-belt)

bandit **tú-fěi**

bank for money **yín-háng** (silver-firm)

bank of river **hé-àn** (river-shore): north bank **běi-àn**

barber, hairdresser **lǐ-fǎ-djyàng** (fix-hair-craftsman)

barber shop **lǐ-fǎ-dyàn** (fix-hair-shop)

bargain, cheap **pyán-yi**

bargain sale **dǎ-djyǎn-djyà** (big-subtract-price)

bargain, haggle **hwán-djyà** (return-price)

barracks **yíng-fáng** (quarters-house)

barrel, tub, pail **tǔng-dz** (*also* hollow cylinder)

barrel of gun **chyăng-gwăn** (gun-tube); barrel of artillery
 piece **pău-gwăn** (cannon-tube)
base position **yuán-dyăn** (origin-point)
base-plate **dí-băn** (bottom-board)
basket **lán-dz**
bathe, take a bath **shí-dzău** (wash-bath): has bathed **shĭ-**
 lə-dzău (wash-done-bath)
bathhouse, bathroom **shí-dzău-fáng** (wash-bath-house)
battery (for electricity) **dyàn-chír** (electric-pool)
battle **djàn-yĭ** (fight-service)
battlefield **djàn-chăng** (fight-field)
bay, inlet **hăi-wăn** (sea-bend)
bayonet **tsĭr-dāu** (stab-knife)
be, is, are, am **shĭr**: I'm an American **wŏ shĭr Mŏi-gwə-rən**
 (I be America-person), this is a good one **djò-gə shĭr**
 hău-də (this be good-belonging); *not used with simple*
 adjectives: that man is big **nà-gə rén dà** (that person big),
 I'm tired **wŏ lài-lə** (I tired)
beans **dòu-dz**
bear (animal) **shyúng**
bear, endure **shòu-kŭ** (endure-bitter)
bear a child **shēng-hái-dz** (born-child)
bear fruit **djyə̄-gwŏr** (produce-fruit)
beard, face hair **hú-dz**
bearing (of machine) **djóu-chéng** (axle-support)
beat, hit **dă**
beat, defeat **dă-bài** (hit-defeat)
beautiful **hău-kàn** (good-look)
because, because of **yīn-wəi**: because he wants to **yīn-wəi**
 tā yàu (because he want), because of him **yīn-wəi tā**
become **lə** (*tacked-on syllable*, done) *or* **dzwò** (*same as* do):
 he became sick **tā bìng-lə** (he sick-done), he became a
 mechanic **tā dzwò dji-gūng-rən** (he do mechanic)

bed **chwáng**

bedding **pŭ-gai** (spread-cover)

beef **nyóu-ròu** (cattle-meat)

before **yĭ-chyán**: before today **djin-tyan yĭ-chyán** (today before)

beg, ask for **yǎu** (*also* want)

beggar **yǎu-fàn** (ask-food)

begin, start **kāi-shĭr** (open-start)

behind **hòu-byan** (rear-side): behind me **dzài-wŏ-hòu-byan** (located-me-behind), go behind the house **dàu-fáng-dz-hòu-byan chyu** (reach-house-behind go)

believe, trust **shìn**: I believe you **wŏ shìn-nĭ**, I don't believe what he says **tā-shwŏ-də wŏ bú-shìn** (he-speak-belonging I not-believe)

bell **djūng** (*also* clock)

belly **dù-dz**

belong **də** (*tacked-on syllable*, belonging): this one belongs to me **djə̀-gə shìr wŏ-də** (this be me-belonging)

below **dĭ-shya** (bottom-down): go below **dàu-dĭ-shya chyù** (reach-below go)

belt, strap, tape **dài-dz** (*sounds like* bag): cartridge belt **dzĭr-dàn-dài**, waist belt **yāu-dai**

bend, to bend **wăn**

best **dzwòi-hău** (most-good)

better **hău-yi-dyar** (good-one-bit)

between **djĭr-djyăn** (between-space): between you and him **dzài-nĭ gēn-tā djĭr-djyăn** (located-you with-him between-space)

bicycle **dzĭr-shíng-chē** (self-move-vehicle)

big **dà**

bigger **dà-yi-dyar** (big-one-bit)

biggest **dzwòi-dà** (most-big)

bill, statement **djàng-dān-dz** (account-list)

bill, banknote **chyán-pyàu-dz** (money-ticket)

bird **nyǎu** *or* **nyǎur**

birthday **shēng-rìr** (born-day)

bite **yǎu**

bitter **kǔ**

black, dark **hēi**

blackboard **hēi-bǎn**

blade **dāu-pyàn** (knife-sheet)

blade of saw **djyù-tyáu** (saw-strip)

blame **gwài**: blame him **gwài-tā**, he's to blame for this matter **djè-gə shìr-ching gwài-tā** (this matter blame-him)

blanket **tǎn-dz**

bleed **lyóu-shyǒ** (flow-blood)

blister **pàu** (*also* bubble)

block, lump **kwài**: iron block **tyǒ-kwài**, wood block **mù-kwài**, a block of ice **yǐ-kwài bīng** (one-lump ice)

blood **shyǒ**

bloom, blossom **kāi-hwā** (open-flower)

blow breath, puff **chwēi**

blow (wind), windy **yǒu-fēng** (have-wind)

blue **lán**

bluff, cliff **shyuǎn-yái**

blunt, dull **dùn**

boards **bǎn-dz**

boat, ship **chwán**

body **shēn-ti**: vehicle body **chē-shēn**

boil, sore **chwāng** (*sounds like* window)

boil (food) **djǔ**; boil (water) **kāi** (*sounds like* open); boiling water **kāi-shwěi**, boiled water for drinking **lyáng-kāi-shwěi** (cool-boil-water)

bolt **lwò-sir** (spiral-strand)

bomb **djà-dàn** (explode-shell), to bomb **hūng-djà** (bombardment-explode) bomber plane **hŭng-djà-djĭ** (bombardment-explode-machine)

bone **gú-təu** (bone-head)

book **shū**

bookkeeper **gwǎn-djàng-də** (manage-account-belonging)

born **shŏng**: I was born in Shanghai **wŏ shŏng dzài-Shàng-hǎi** (I born located-Shanghai)

borrow **djyà**: I want to borrow money from you **wŏ yàu gŏn-nǐ djyà-chyán** (I want with-you borrow-money)

boss, foreman **gŭng-tóu** (work-head)

both **dŏu** (_same as_ all): they are both well **tǎ-mən lyǎng-gə dŏu-hǎu** (they two all-good)

bother, disturb **má-fan**: don't bother him **byà má-fan-ta**

bottle **píng-dz**: a bottle of wine **yǐ-píng djyŏu** (one-bottle wine)

bottom **dǐ**

boundary **gwó-djyà** (country-border)

bow (with joined hands) **dzwŏ-yǐ** (make-bow); bow low **djyú-gŭng** (bend-torso); bow and nod **dyǎn-tóu** (nod-head)

bowl **wǎn**: a bowl of rice **yǐ-wǎn fàn** (one-bowl rice)

bowling, to bowl **pāu-chyóu** (cast-ball)

box (large) **shyäng-dz** (_also_ trunk, suitcase); small box **hó-dz**: three boxes of books **sān-shyäng shū** (three-case book), three boxes of matches **sān-hó yáng-hwŏ** (three-box match)

boy **nán-hái-dz** (male-child)

brakes **shā-chŏ** (brake-vehicle)

branch **shù-djir-dz** (tree-branch)

branch office **fŏn-háng** (division-firm)

brass **hwáng-túng** (yellow-copper)

brave **yúng-gǎn**

bread **myàn-bāu** (flour-package)

break by bending **djyuŏ-dwàn** (bend-snap): break into a

few pieces **dǎ-pwə̀** (hit-break), break up, shatter, smash **dǎ-swə̀i** (hit-fragments)

break down, get out of order **hwǎi-lə** (*same as* spoiled)

breakfast **dzǎu-fàn** (early-food)

breathe **hū-shi** (exhale-inhale)

bride, bridegroom **shìn-rə́n** (new-person)

bridge **chyáu**

bridle, halter, reins **djyǎng-shəng**

briefcase **shū-bāu** (book-package)

bright, clever **tsūng-ming**

bright, shiny **lyàng**

bring **dài-lai** (lead-come) *or* **ná-lai** (pickup-come): bring the horses here **dài-mǎ lai** (lead-horse come), bring food **ná-fàn lai** (pickup-food come)

British Empire **Dà-yìng-dì-gwə́** (Big-English-empire)

broad, wide **kwǎn**

broil **bāu** (*sounds like* package, wrap)

broom **sàu-ba** (sweep-instrument, *understood everywhere but Peiping area*) *or* **sàu-chəu** (*in Peiping area*)

brothers **shyüng-dì**; older brother **gə̄-gə**; younger brother **dì-di**

brown **dzūng-sə̀-də** (palm-color-belonging)

brush **shwā-dz**, to brush **shwā**

brush, Chinese writing instrument **bǐ** (*sounds like* compare)

bubble **pàu** (*sounds like* cannon)

bucket, tub, barrel **tǔng** (*also* hollow cylinder)

buffalo **shwǒi-nyə́u** (water-cattle)

bug, insect **chúng-dz**

build, construct **dzàu**: they build a factory **tā-mən dzàu gūng-chǎng**

bulb (electric light) **də̄ng-pàu** (lamp-bubble)

bull, ox **gūng-nyə́u** (male-cattle)

bullet **dzǐr-dàn** (son-shell)

bunch (held together) **kŭn**, bunch, group **chyún**: a bunch of
   flowers **yĭ-kŭn hwā** (one-bunch flower), a bunch of people
   yĭ-chyún rə́n (one-group person)
Buddhism **fwə́-djyàu** (Buddha-teaching)
building, house **fáng-dz**; tall building **lə́u**
bump **pə̀ng**
Burma **Myǎn-dyàn**
burn **hwə̌-shāng** (fire-injury)
burn, heat, roast **shāu**
burning, afire **djáu-lə**
burst **bǎu-lə**
bus **gūng-gùng chĭ-chə̄** (public automobile)
bus stop **chĭ-chə̄-djàn** (automobile-stop)
bushes **tsúng-shù** (group-tree)
business, commerce **mǎi-mai** (buy-sell)
busy **yǒu-shĭr** (have-work)
but **kə̌-shir**: I want to go but I'm not allowed to **wə̌ yàu
   chyù kə̌-shir bù-kə́-yi chyù** (I want go but not-allowed go)
butcher **mài-rə̀u-də** (sell-meat-belonging)
butcher shop **rə̀u-dyàn** (meat-shop)
butter **nyə́u-yə́u** (cow-oil) *or* **hwáng-yə́u** (yellow-oil)
buttons **kə̀u-dz**
buy **mǎi**
by **yùng** (*same as* use) *or* **dzwə̀** (*same as* sit): he does it with
   a knife **tā yùng-dāu-dz dzwə̀** (he use-knife do), he comes
   by plane **tā dzwə̀-fə̄i-djī lái** (he sit-airplane come)

C

cabbage **bái-tsài** (white-food)
cabinet (furniture) **gwə̀i-dz**
cable, wire **shyàn** (*also* thread)
call out, shout **dǎ-shə̄ng djyàu** (big-sound call)

called, to call **djyàu** (*also* tell to do): what is this thing called in Chinese? **djə̀-gə dŭng-shi Djŭng-gwə-hwà djyàu shə́m-mə** (this thing China-words called what)

calm, collected, steady **djə̀n-djing**

camera **djàu-shyàng-djî** (shine-picture-machine)

camouflage **wə̌i-djwăng** (false-pretend)

camp, bivouac **lù-yíng** (expose-camp)

can **hwə̀i** (knowing how to) *or* **nə́ng** (able to) *or* **kə́-yi** (possible, maybe): he can drive a car but isn't allowed to **tă hwə̀i kāi chî-chə̂ kə̌-shir bù-kə́-yi kăi**, I can't lift it by myself **wə̌ yí-gə-rən bù-nə́ng bă-ta tái-chi-lai** (I one-person not-able take-it raise-up-come), it can happen **kə́-yi chŭ-shìr** (possible happen)

can, container **gwăn-tə́u** (container-head): one can of **yí-gwăn**, three cans **săn-gə gwăn-tə́u** (three-item can), three cans of fruit **săn-gwăn shwə́i-gwə̌** (three-container fruit)

canal **yùn-hə́** (transport-river)

candle **là** (*same as* wax)

candy **táng** (*also* sugar)

cannon, artillery piece **pàu** (*sounds like* bubble)

canteen **shwə̌i-hú** (water-pot, *same as* kettle)

canvas, tarpaulin **fán-bù** (sail-cloth)

cap, hat **màu-dz**

capital city **djing-chə́ng**

capital investment **bə̌n-chyan** (root-money)

captain **shàng-wə̀i** (upper-companyofficer)

capture **fú-lwə̌** (*also* prisoner); capture (supplies) **fú-hwə̀** (capture-goods)

car, cart, vehicle **chə̂**: motor car **chî-chə̂** (gas-vehicle)

carburetor **chî-hwà-djî** (gas-evaporate-machine)

card **kă-pyàn** *or* **chyă-pyàn** (card-sheet): calling card **míng-pyàn** (name-sheet) cards **pŭ-kə̀-pái** (poker-domino, *but used for all kinds of playing cards*); to play cards **dá-djìr-pái** (hit-paper-domino)

careful **shyăn-shin** (small-heart): be careful with that gun **shyăn-shin nə̀-gə chyăng** (careful that gun)

careless **tsŭ-shin** (coarse-heart)

carpet, rug **dì-tăn** (ground-blanket) *or* **shí-dz** (*same as* mat)

carry **ná-chyu** (pickup-go): carry a basket **ná-lán-dz chyu** (pickup-basket go)

cartridge **chyăng-dàn** (gun-shell)

cash **shyàn-chyán** (cash-money)

casualties **shăng-wáng** (wound-dead)

cat **mău**

catch, stopping pin **kə̀u** (*same as* button)

catch, capture **djwə̆**

catch hold **djwă**

catch in the air **djyə̆** (*also* accept)

Catholic **Tyăn-djŭ-də** (Catholic-belonging): a Catholic **Tyăn-djŭ**, Catholic church **Tyăn-djŭ-táng** (Catholic-hall)

Catholicism **Tyăn-djŭ-djyàu** (Catholic-teaching)

cattle (beef animal) **nyə́u**

cattle, livestock **shə̄ng-kəu** (creature-mouth)

cavalry, cavalryman **chí-bing** (straddle-soldier)

celebrate **chìng-dju**

celebration **hwə̀i** (*also* party, meeting)

censor, inspect, censorship, inspection **djyăn-chá** (examine-investigate)

cent **fə̄n-chyán** (division-money): five cents **wŭ-fə̄n-chyán**

center **djŭng-djyăn** (middle-space)

center of balance **djùng-shin** (weight-heart)

central **djŭng-yăng** (middle-manner)

centimeter **gŭng-fə̄n** (universal-division): one centimeter **yì-gŭng-fə̄n** certainly, definitely **yí-dìng** (one-settled)

chain **lyàn-dz**

chair **yǐ-dz**

chairman **djǔ-shí** (chief-position)

chalk **fén-bǐ** (powder-brush *or* powder-writinginstrument)

change, exchange, trade **hwàn**: changes his money **hwàn tä-də chyán**, money given in change **hwàn-chyán** (change-money)

change, small coins **líng-chyán** (sundry-money)

change condition **byàn-lə**: the color changes **yán-sə byàn-lə**

character, nature **shùng-djir** (nature-quality)

character, written sign **dzìr**

charge, buy on credit **shə̄**; charge account **djàng**: charge it **kāi-djàng** (open-account)

charge, attack **chǔng-fə̄ng** (rush-spearhead)

chart, table **byǎu** (*also* watch)

chase **djwə̄i** (trying to catch) *or* **gǎn** (driving away)

chassis **dǐ-djyà** (bottom-frame)

cheap, low-priced **pyán-yi**

cheat **chī-pyàn**

check **djir-pyàu** (cash-ticket)

check up **kàn-yi-kan** (look-one-look): check this **kàn-yi-kan djə̄-gə dwə̄i-bu-dwə̄i** (look-one-look this correct-not-correct)

checkers **chí** (*also* chess *and other similar games*)

cheerful, happy **gāu-shìng** (high-spirits)

cheese **chì-sir** (*like English*)

chest, thorax **shyüng**

chest, trunk, box **shyäng-dz**

chicken **djī**: chicken meat **djī-rə̀u**

chief **lǐng-shyə̀u** (*same as* leader) *or* **djǎng-gwǎn** (chief-officer)

chief, most important **dzwə̀i-dà-də** (most big-belonging)

child **shyǎu-hái-dz** (small-child, *sounds like* small-shoe *in some parts of China*): small child, baby **shyáu shyǎu-hái-dz**
China **Djüng-gwə** (middle-country)
Chinese **Djüng-gwə-də** (China-belonging): Chinese language **Djüng-gwə-hwà**, Chinese person **Djüng-gwə-rə́n** (China-person)
chinaware, porcelain **tsir-chǐ**
cholera **hwə́-lwàn**
chop (with axe) **kǎn**
chop up, mince up **dwə̀**
chopsticks **kwài-dz**
Christian **Dji-du-də** (Christ-belonging): Christian religion **Dji-du-djyàu** (Christ-teaching)
church **lǐ-bài-táng** (worship-hall)
cigarette **shyāng-yǎn** (fragrant-tobacco)
cinch (harness) **dù-dài** (belly-belt)
circle **yuán-chyuān** (round-loop)
circuit **dyàn-lù** (electric-road)
citizen **shìr-mín** (city-people)
city **chə́ng**
civilian **láu-bǎi-shìng** (old-hundred-surname)
clamp **djyā-dz** (squeeze-article)
class, quality **dǒng**: first class **yǐ-dǒng** (one-class)
clean **gān-djing** (dry-clear)
clear, understandable **chǐng-chu** (clear-exit)
clear, unmuddied **chǐng** (*sounds like* fresh, lightweight)
clear space **kùngr**
clear the way **dǎ-kāi yǐ-tyáu lù** (beat-open one-strip road)
clear weather **chǐng-tyān** (fair-day)
clerk in store **hwə́-dji** (*also* waiter); record clerk **shū-dji** (book-record)
clever, smart **tsūng-ming**
cliff, bluff **shyuán-yái**

climb **pá-shàng** (climb-up): he climbs the hill **tā pá-shàng shān**

climb, gain altitude **shàng-shēng** (up-ascend): the airplane climbs **fēi-dji shàng-shēng**

clip (for papers) **djǐr-byé-dz** (paper-clasp)

clip for ammunition **dàn-djyǎ** (bullet-case)

clippers (barber's) **lǐ-fà-də twəi-dz** (arrange-hair-belonging push-thing)

clock **djūng** (*also* bell): clockwise **shùn djūng-byǎu fāng shyàng** (along clock-watch direction-towards), counterclockwise **fǎn djūng-byǎu fāng-shyàng** (reverse clockwise)

close by **dzài-fù-djìn** (located-attach-near)

close (door), turn off (light) **gwān**

cloth **bù**; woolen cloth **ní** (*sounds like* mud)

clothes **yī-shang** (clothing-garment)

cloud **yún-tsai**

club, stick **gǎn-dz**

club, social organization **djyù-lə̀-bù** (together-joyful-section)

clutch (on a car) **lí-hé-chǐ** (apart-together-device)

coal **méi**

coast, seashore **hǎi-àn** (sea-shore)

coat **shàng-yī** (upper-clothing)

code, cipher **mì-mǎ** (secret-figures); Morse code **dyàn-mǎ** (electric-figures)

coffee **kā-fēi** *or* **djyā-fēi**

coils **shyàn-chyuān** (wire-loop)

cold **lěng**

cold, catarrh, to catch cold **shāng-fēng** (injury-wind)

collar **lǐng-dz**

collect **shēu-djí** (gather-assemble)

college **dà-shyué** (big-study)

colonel **shàng-shyàu** (upper-fieldgrade)

color **yán-sə**

comb **shū-dz**

combat, fighting **djàn-dǝu** (fight-wrangle)

come **lái**; come back **hwǝi-lai** (return-come); come in **djǐn-lai** (enter-come); come out **chū-lai** (exit-come)

come together, converge **hwǝi-hǝ́** (meet-together)

comfortable, relaxed **shū-fu**

command, to command **mǐng-ling**

commanding officer **djǎng-gwǎn** (senior-officer)

committee **wǒi-yuán-hwǝi** (commission-personnel-meet)

common, ordinary **pǔ-tūng**: the common man **pǔ-tūng-rǝ́n**, that is very common in China **nà-gǝ dzài-djūng-gwǝ hǝ́n-pǔ-tūng** (that located-China very-common)

communicate, communication **tūng-shǐn** (communicate-message)

company, business house **shāng-háng** (commerce-firm)

company, guests **kǝ̀-rən** (courtesy-person)

company of soldiers **lyán**

compare **bǐ**: this doesn't compare with that **djǝ̀-gǝ bù-nǝ́ng bǐ-nà-gǝ** (this not-able compare-that), compare this one with that one **bǎ-djǝ̀-gǝ gǝ̄n-nà-gǝ bǐ-yi-bi** (take-this with-that compare-one-compare)

compass **djǐr-nán-djǝ̄n** (point-south-needle)

complain, complain about **bǎu-yuan** (embrace-complaint)

complete, finish **wán-lǝ**: he completed the work **tā dzwǝ̀-wán-lǝ shìr-lǝ** (he do-finish-done job-done), the job is complete **shyàn-dzài shìr dzwǝ̀-wán-lǝ** (now job do-finish-done)

compressed, to compress **yǎ-swǝ̄** (press-shrink)

concave **wǎ-dǝ** (cavity-belonging)

concealment, to conceal **yǐn-bǐ** (conceal-hide)

concern, business house **shāng-háng** (commerce-firm)

concerning **dàu** (*same as* reach): concerning this matter **dàu-djǝ̀-gǝ shìr-ching** concrete **shwǒi-ní** (water-mud)

condenser (electrical) **dyǎn-rúng-chǐ** (electric-contain-device)

cone **djwǒi-tǐ** (cone-body)

Confucianism **Kúng-djyǎu** (Confucius-teaching)

Confucius **Kúng-dzǐr**

connect **dyjǝ-chi-lai** (receive-up-come)

continent **dǎ-djǝu** (big-continent)

continue **djǐ-shyù**

control, govern **kùng-djìr** (subject-govern)

control, manage (people, affairs) **gwǎn**

controls **kùng-djìr dji-gwǎn** (control machine-shut)

convenient **fāng-byan** (direction-convenience)

convex **gǔ-də** *or* **tù-də** (protrude-belonging)

cook, chef **chú-dz**

cook food **dzwǒ-fàn** (make-food)

cook in water, boil, stew **djǔ**

cool **lyáng**: weather is cool **tyǎn-chi lyáng-kwai** (weather cool-comfortable)

coolie **kǔ-lì** (bitter-strength, *not a respectful word and, it's sometimes more tactful to say* workman, **gūng-rən**)

copper **túng**

copy, duplicate **fù-djǎng** (secondary-sheet)

copy off, make a copy **chāu**

core **tyǒ-shin** (iron-heart)

corner, angle **djyǎu** (*sounds like* foot) *or* **djyuǒ**: corner of a room **wū-djyǎu** (room-angle)

corner (of streets), intersection **djyǒ-kǒu** (street-mouth)

corporal **shyǎ-shìr** (lower-noncom)

correct, make right **gǎi-djǒng** (alter-upright)

correct, right **dwǒi-lə**

cotton wadding **myán-hwa** (cotton-flower); medical cotton **yǎu-myán** (medicine-cotton)

count up **shǔ**

counter-attack **fǎn-gūng** (reverse-attack)

courtesy **lǐ-màu** (ceremony-manners)

country, land **dì**

country, nation **gwó-djyā** (country-family)

court of law **fǎ-yuàn**

cover, lid **gài-dz**; to cover over **gài-shang** (cover-on)

cow, cattle, bull, ox **nyóu**

crank **shǒu-yáu-bǐng** (hand-rock-handle)

crawl **pá**

crayon **là-bǐ** (wax-brush)

crazy **fōng-lə**

credentials **djàng-shū** (certificate-book)

credit **shō-djàng** (charge-account) *or* **shō**: he buys on credit **tā shō-djàng** (he charge-account), he buys a hat on credit **tā shō yì-dǐng màu-dz** (he charge one-top hat)

crew, personnel **rén-yuán** (person-operator)

criticize, find fault **pi-ping**

crooked, curved, bent **wān-də** (bend-belonging)

crops **djwāng-djya** (farm-plants)

cross **shír-dzìr** (ten-character—*the Chinese writing for* ten *has the shape of a cross*)

cross over **gwò**: come across **gwò-lai** (cross-come), go across **gwò-chyu** (cross-go)

cross section **dwàn-myàn** (sever-surface)

crosswise **háng**

crow **wū-yā**

cry, weep **kū**

crystal **djing-tǐ** (crystal-body)

culvert **hán-dùng** (soak-tunnel)

cup **bēi-dz** (*also* drinking glass): a cup of coffee **yì-bēi kā-fēi** (one-cup coffee)

current **lyóu**: electric current **dyàn-lyóu**, water current **shwěi-lyóu**

curve, bend **wǎn**
curved, crooked, bent **wǎn-də** (bend-belonging)
cushion, pad **dyàn-dz**
cut **chyɔ̌**
cylinder (hollow) **tǔng** (*also* barrel, pail)
cylinder (solid) **yuán-djù-tǐ** (round-pillar-body)
cylinder of gas engine **chì-gāng** (gas-jar)

D

dam **shwɔ̌i-djá** (water-dam)
damp, wet **shīr** (*sounds like* army division)
dance **tyàu-wǔ** (jump-dance)
dangerous **wɔ́i-shyǎn**
dark (without light) **hēi** (*same as* black): it's turned dark, become night **tyǎn hēi-lə** (sky dark-done)
dark-colored **shēn** (*same as* deep) *or* **shēn-yǎn-sə-də** (deep-color-belonging): dark red **shēn-húng**
daughter **nyǔ-ər** (female-son)
day **tyǎn** (*also* sky): one day **yì-tyǎn**
daytime **bái-tyan** (white-sky)
dead, to die **sǐr-lə**
debt **djài**
decide **djyuɔ́-dìng** (determine-settled): he decides to go **tā djyuɔ́-dìng chyù** (he decide go)
deck of ship **djyá-bǎn** (shell-board)
decode, decipher **fān-yi mì-mǎ** (translate secret-figures)
deep **shēn**
deer **lù** (*sounds like* road)
defeat **dǎ-bài** (hit-defeat)
defend **fáng-yù** (prevent-resist)
definite, certain **yí-dìng** (one-settled)
degree **dù**: how many degrees? **dwɔ̌-shǎu-dù**, thirty degrees **sān-shir-dù**

delay **dăn-wu**

dentist **yǎ-yî** (tooth-cure)

department, part **bù-fən** (section-division)

department store **băi-hwə̀-gŭng-sîr** (hundred-goods-concern)

deposit, down payment, to pay down **shyăn-fù** (first-pay)

deposit money (in bank) **tsún-chyán** (store-money)

desert **shă-mwə̀** (sand-waste)

desk **shŭ-djwə̌** (book-table)

dessert **dyăn-shin** (dot-heart)

destroy **pwə̀-hwài** (break-spoiled)

details **shyáng-chíng** (detailed-condition)

develop, grow **fā-djăn** (issue-extend)

develop films **shǐ-shyàng-pyăr** (wash-films)

diagonal line **dwə̀i-djyău-shyàn** (opposite-angle-line)

diagram, sketch **tú-hwà** (picture-drawing)

dial **bwə̌-hàu-pán** (shift-number-plate)

diameter **djír-djìng** (straight-distance)

diarrhea **shyə̀-dù-dz** (spill-belly)

dictionary **dzìr-dyăn** (word-rule)

die, dead **sǐr-lə**

different **bù-yí-yàng** (not-one-manner)

differential **chă-sù-chǐ** (differ-speed-device)

difficult **nán**

dig **wā**

dinner at noon, lunch **wǔ-fàn** (noon-food)

dinner at night, supper **wăn-fàn** (evening-food)

diplomat **wài-djyău-gwăn** (outside-contact-officer)

dipper, ladle **shău-dz**

direct **djír-djyə̌** (straight-connect)

direction **byăn** (*same as* side): go in that direction **wàng-nà-byan dzə̌u** (towards-that-side walk)

dirt, soil **tǔ**

dirty **dzăng-lə**

dish, plate **pán-dz**

discharge (employee) **kăi-shyău-lə** (open-cancel-done)

discharge (weapon) **kăi** (*same as* open)

discipline **djĭ-lyù** (orderliness-law)

disease, sickness, sick **bìng**

disinfectant **shyău-dú-yàu** (erase-poison-medicine)

disorder **hùn-lwàn** (mix-confusion)

dispensary **wài-shēn-swá** (guard-body-structure)

distributor (in gas-engine) **pài-dyàn-chĭ** (match-electricity-device)

disturb **má-fan**

ditch **gōu** (*also* gully)

dive (airplane loses altitude quickly) **fú-chŭng** (dive-rush)

dive into water **tyàu-shwăi** (jump-water)

divide, separate **fēn-kai** (division-open)

division, part **bù-fən** (section-division)

division (army unit) **shĭr** (*sounds like* wet)

do, make **dzwà** (*sounds like* sit)

dock **chwán-wŭ** (boat-wall)

doctor **yĭ-shəng** (heal-person)

document, papers **wén-dyàn** (document-articles)

dog **gōu**

dollar **kwài-chyán** (lump-money): a dollar **yí-kwài-chyán** (one-lump-money), three dollars **sān-kwài-chyán**

donkey **lyú-dz**

don't **byá** *or* **bú-yàu** (not-want): don't do that **byá nà-yang** (don't that-manner), don't come **byá-lái**

door **mén** (*also* gate)

double **shwăng-də** (pair-belonging)

down, get down from **shyà**: go down **shyà-chyu** (down-go), get down from the wagon **shyà-chē** (down-vehicle), downstairs **lóu-shyà** (building-down), we walked down-stream **wś-mən shùn-dj hś shyȧng-shyȧ dzȘu** (us along-side river towards-down walk), the boat went down-stream **chwȧn shyȧ-shwȘi dzȘu** (boat down-water go)

down payment, to pay down **shyān-fù** (first-pay)

draft of air **chȉ-lyśu** (air-current)

draft of money **hwȿi-pyȧu** (send-ticket)

draftsman **hwȿi-tú-yuán** (draw-map-personnel)

drag, tow **twȝ**

drain **fȧng-shwȘi** (release-water): drain pipe **fȧng-shwȘi-gwȧn**, drain plug **fȧng-shwȘi-sāi**

draw, paint **hwȧ** (*also* a picture)

dream **mȿng**, to dream **dzwȿ-mȿng** (make-dream)

dress, skirt **chyún-dz**

dress up **chwȧn-chi yȉ-shang lai** (dress-up clothes come)

drill (tool) **dzwȧn-dz;** to drill holes in **dzwȧn**

drill, do military exercises **tsāu-yȧn** (exercise-train)

drill, practice up **lyȧn-shȉ** (train-practice)

drink **hȝ**: drink water **hȝ-shwȘi**, drink wine **hȝ-djyȘu**

drive (car, motorcycle, etc.) **kāi** (*same as* open)

drive (animals), chase away **gȧn**

driver of auto or locomotive **sȉr-djȉ** (control-machine)

driver of wagon **gȧn-chȝ-də** (drive-vehicle-belonging)

driver of pack animals **twś-fu** (pack-fellow)

drop down **dyȧu-shya-lai** (drop-down-come)

drugs, medicine **yȧu**

drugstore (modern type) **yȧu-fȧng** (medicine-house); old-style drugstore **yȧu-tsár-pù** (medicine-material-store)

drum, barrel, pail **tǔng** (*same as* hollow cylinder)

drum for music **gǔ** (*sounds like* valley)

drunk, intoxicated **dzwȿi-lə**

dry, dried out **gȧn-lə**: weather is dry **tyȧn-chi gȧn-dzȧu** (weather dry-parched)

dryclean **gȧn-shȉ** (dry-wash)

dry-goods store **djǐng-hwở-pù** (Peking-goods-store) *or* **mǎi-
    yǐ-lyǎu-də pù-dz** (sell-clothing-material-belonging store)
duck **yǎ-dz**
dummy, fake **djyǎ-də**
dull, blunt **dùn**
dung **shǐr**
dust **hwǝi-chǝn**
duties **djǐr-wù** (duties-business)
dutiful, diligent **djǐn-dzǒ** (fulfil-duty)
duty **dzǒ-rǝn** (duty-responsibility)
dyes, paints **yán-lyǎu** (color-stuff)
dynamite **dǎi-ná-mǎi-tə** (*from English*)
dynamo, generator **fā-dyǎn-djī** (issue-electricity-machine)
dysentery **lǐ-dji** (purge-disease)

E

each, every **mǒi-gə** (each-item): each person **mǒi-gə rǒn**,
    each year **mǒi-nyán**
ear **ǒr-dəu**
earphone **tǐng-tǔng** (listen-cylinder)
early **dzǎu**
earth, dirt **tǔ**
earth, land **dǐ**; the earth **dǐ-chyǒu** (earth-ball)
east **dūng**: in the east **dzài-dūng-byan** (located-east-side),
    towards the east **shyàng-dūng-byan** (toward-east-side)
easy **rúng-yi**
eat **chǐr**: eat meat **chǐr-rǒu**, he has eaten **tā chǐr-lə fàn-lə**
    (he eat-done food-done)
education **djyàu-yu** (teach-principle)
effect, result **djyǒ-gwǒ** (yield-fruit)
egg **dàn** (*sounds like* bullet): chicken egg **djī-dàn**
eight **bā**

eighth **dǐ-bă-gə** (sequence-eight-item); one eighth **bă-fən-dj yǐ** (eight-division-derived one)

eighty **bă-shir** (eight-ten)

elbow **gə̆-bəi djə̆u-dz** (arm elbow)

elect, election **shyuán-djyǔ** (select-vote)

electricity **dyàn**: electric light **dyàn-dǒng**, electric power **dyàn-lǐ**, electrolyte **dyàn-djyə̆-yə̀** (electricity-loosen-liquid)

elephant **shyàng** (*sounds like* towards *and* resemble)

elevation over sea level **bá-hǎi** (extract-sea): this place has an elevation of 500 meters **djə̀-li bá-hǎi wú-bǎi gǔng-chǐr** (here elevation five-hundred meter)

elevator **dyàn-tǐ** (electric-ladder)

embassy **dà-shír-gwǎn** (ambassador-establishment)

empire **dǐ-gwə́** (emperor-country)

employ, hire **gù**

employee, worker **gǔng-rən** (work-person); employee in a business **háng-yuán** (business-personnel)

empty **kǔng-də**

end, conclusion **djyə́-wǒi** (final-tail)

end of an object **tə́ur**: front end **chyán-təu**, rear end **hə̀u-təu**

enemy country **dí-gwə́**; the enemy **dí-rə́n** (enemy-person); enemy area **dí-chyǔ**

engine, motor **fă-dùng-dji** (issue-move-machine) *or* **dji-chǐ** (*same as* machine)

engine driver, chauffeur **sǐr-dji** (control-machine)

engineer, expert in engineering **gǔng-chə́ng-shǐr** (work-distance-master)

engineer (army) **gǔng-bing** (work-soldier)

England **Yǐng-gwə** (Eng-country)

English **Yǐng-gwə-də** (England-belonging): Englishman **Yǐng-gwə-rən** (England-person), English language **Yǐng-gwə-hwà** (England-words) enjoy, like **shǐ-hwan**; enjoys oneself **wán-də hə́n-hǎu** (play-belonging very-good): I enjoy books **wə́ shǐ-hwan shū**, we enjoy ourselves **wə́-mən-wán-də́ hə́n-hǎu** (we-play-belonging very-good)

enlisted man, plain soldier **bīng**

envelope **shìn-fə̄ng** (letter-seal)

equal **píng-də̌ng** (level-class): you are equal to him **nǐ gə̄n-ta píng-də̌ng** (you with-him equal)

error **tswə̀-wu** (mistake-wrong)

escape **táu**

estimate **gǔ-djǐ**

Europe **ə̌u-djəu** (Eu-continent)

even if **djyə̀u-shir**: even if he spoke **tā djyə̀u-shir shwə̀-hwà** (he even speak-word)

evening (after dark) **wǎn-shang** (late-on); early evening **shyà-wǔ** (*same as* afternoon)

every, each **mə̌i-gə**: everyone **mə̌i-gə-rən** (each-item-person), every day **mə̌i-tyǎn**, every year **mə̌i-nyán**

exact, accurate **djǔn-chyuə̀**: the exact amount **chyuə̀-shù** (exact-number)

exactly **chyà-chyà**

example **lǐ-dz** (*sounds like* chestnut); for example **lǐ-rú** (example-like)

except **chú-lə**: all except him want to come **chú-lə-tā də̄u yə̀u-lái** (except-him all want-come)

exchange **hwàn**

excited **hwāng-lə**

excuse, pretext **twə̀i-twə** (push-pretext)

excuse me, I'm sorry **dwə̀i-bu-chǐ** (face-not-up)

exhaust pipe **pái-chǐ-gwǎn** (dispose-gas-tube)

expect **shyǎng** (*same as* think): I expect them to come **wə́-shyǎng tā-mən yə̀u-lái** (I-think they will-come)

expensive **gwə̀i**

expert **djwăn-djyă** (special-ist): an expert mechanic **dji-chĭ djwăn-djyă** (machine expert)

explain **djyŏ-shĭr** (solve-clarify)

explode **djă**

explosives (high) **djă-yău** (explode-medicine); low explosives **hwŏ-yău** (fire-medicine)

extra, spare **băi-yung-də** (prepare-use-belonging)

eye **yăn-djing**

F

face **lyăn**

face of an object, surface **myàn**

facing, towards **shyàng** (*sounds like* like, resemble): stands facing me **shyàng-wŏ djàn-dj** (towards-me stand-remain)

factory **gūng-chăng** (work-factory)

fake, counterfeit **djyă-də** (false-belonging)

fall of the year **chyŏu-tyan** (autumn-day)

fall, drop **dyàu-shya-lai** (drop-down-come); fall over, topple **shwāi-dău**

false, not so **bú-shĭr** (not-be) *or* **bú-shĭr djən-də** (not-be true)

false, fake **djă-də**; false, artificial **făng-dzău-də** (imitate-construct-belonging)

family **djyă** (*same as* home)

famous **yŏu-míng** (have-name)

fan **shàn-dz**, to fan **shān** (*sounds like* hill): engine fan **fēng-shàn** (wind-fan)

far **yuăn**

farmer **djùng-dĭ-də** (cultivate-land-belonging) *or* **núng-rən** (farming-person)

farmland, to farm **djùng-dĭ** (cultivate-land)

fast, quick **kwài** (*also* sharp-pointed): he talks fast **tā-shwŏ-**

dǝ kwài (he-talk-belonging fast), the clock is fast djūng kwài (clock fast)

fat, stout, fleshy pàng; fatty (nickname etc.) pàng-dz

fat (of meat) fǝi: fat meat fǝi-rǝu

father fù-chin

fault, mistake tswǝ-wu *or* tswǝr: it's my fault shìr wǒ-dǝ tswǝr (be me-belonging mistake)

fear, to be afraid of pà

feed, fodder tsǎu-lyàu (grass-grain)

feed (animals) wǝi; feed (people) gǝi-fàn chìr (give-food eat)

feel by touch mwǝ

feel a certain way djyuǝ-dǝ: I feel badly about that yin-wǝi nà-gǝ shìr wǒ djyuǒ-dǝ bù-hǎu (because that matter I feel not-good)

female nyǚ: female person nyǚ-rǝn; female (of animals) mǔ-dǝ (female-belonging)

fence, wall chyáng; wire fence tyǒ-sìr-wǎng (iron-strand-net); woven bamboo fence djú-lí-ba (bamboo-hedge)

fender, mudguard ní-hù-dz (mud-guard-thing)

ferry dù-chwán (ford-boat)

feverish fā-shāu (issue-burn *or* issue-fever)

few, a small number shǎu-shù-dǝ (little-number-belonging); a few, several djǐ-gǝ (*also used for* how many)

field, open area kǔng-chǎng (empty-field): airfield fǝi-dji-chǎng (fly-machine-field)

field, cultivated land tyán

fifth dì-wǔ-gǝ (sequence-five-item), one fifth wǔ-fǝn-dj yi (five-division-derived one)

fifty wǔ-shir (five-ten)

fight a battle dǎ-djàng (hit-combat); fight, brawl dǎ-djyà (hit-frame)

figure, shape yàng-dz; figure, build (of a person) shǝn-tsái (body-style)

figure out **shyǎng-chu-lai** (think-out-come): he can't figure
out a plan **tā shyǎng-bu-chū yí-gə djǐ-hwa lai** (he think-
not-out one plan come)

figure up **swàn-chu-lai** (calculate-out-come): he figures up
the amount **tā bǎ-shù-mu swàn-chu-lai** (he take-amount
figure-out-come)

file for records **dǎng-àn** (section-records)

file (steel tool) **tswə̀-dz**

fill up **djwāng-mǎn** (fill-full)

filling station **chǐ-yə́u-djàn** (gas-oil-station)

film roll **djyāu-djyuǎn** (glue-roll); flat film **djyāu-pyàn**
(glue-card)

films, movies **dyàn-yǐng** (electric-shadow)

filter **lyù-chǐ** (strain-device): oil filter **lyù-yə́u-chǐ** (strain-
oil-device), radio filter **lyù-bwə̀-chǐ** (strain-wave-device)

find **djǎu-dàu** (seek-reach) *or* **djǎu-djáu-lə**

finely ground **shǐ**

finger **shə́u-djǐr-təu** (hand-point-end)

finish school, graduate **bǐ-yə̀**

finish up **wán-lə** (finish-done): I finished the work **wə̌**
dzwə̀-wán-lə shǐr-lə (I do-finish-done job-done), I finished digging **wə̌ wā-wán-lə** (I dig-finish-done)

fins **hwá-shwə̌i** (slide-water)

fire, flames **hwə̌**: to set fire **fàng-hwə̌** (letgo-fire)

fire, discharge (firearms) **kāi** (*same as* open); to fire (employee) **kāi-shyāu-lə** (open-cancel-done); he fired a gun
tā kāi-chyāng (him open-gun), he fired me **tā bá-wə̌ kāi-**
shyāu-lə (he take-me open-cancel-done)

firearm **chyāng-pàu** (gun-cannon)

first-aid **djyə̀u-djí** (help-haste)

first one **dǐ-yí-gə** (sequence-one-item); first of all **shyān**:
we'll tell the first one first **wə̌-mən shyān gàu-su dǐ-yí-gə**
rə́n (we first inform sequence-one-item person)

fish **yú**: to fish **dǎ-yú** (hit-fish)

fit (machine parts) together **pèi-hé** (mate-together)

fix up, rebuild **shyóu-li**; fix, mend **bǔ-yi-bu** (patch-one-patch)

flag **chí-dz**

flames **hwǒ-myáu** (fire-sprouts)

flash **shǎn-gwāng** (lighting-illumination)

flashlight **shǒu-dyàn-tǔng** (hand-electric-cylinder)

flat, level, smooth **píng-də**

flexible **néng-wān-də** (able-bend-belonging)

float, be afloat **pyáu**

floor **dì** (*also* ground)

floor, story **tséng**: one floor **yì-tséng**

flour **myàn-fěn** (flour-powder)

flow **lyóu**

flower **hwā**

fly (insect) **tsāng-ying** (darkblue-fly)

fly thru the air **fēi**: flywheel **fēi-lún**

focus **djyāu-dyǎn** (scorched-point)

fog, mist **wù**

follow **gēn-swéi** *or* **gēn** (*also* with): follow me **gēn-wǒ**

food, meal **fàn** (*this word refers mainly to rice and wheat foods*); food-dish of meat or vegetables **tsài**

fool, deceive, trick **shàng-dàng** (up-pawnshop)

fool, idiot **shǎ-dz**

foolish **shǎ**

foot **djyǎu** (*sounds like* angle): footprints **djyǎu-yìn** *or* **djyǎu-yèr**

foot of measure **yìng-chǐr** (English-lengthmeasure), *but the metric system is better known, so use centimeters and meters*

for **gěi** (*same as* give): do it for him **gěi-tā dzwò** (give-him do)

for, in favor of, agree with **dzàn-chéng**

force, strength **lì-chi** (strength-air)

force, violence **wŭ-lì** (military-strength)
force to do **yā-pwə** (press-persecute)
ford in stream **tú-shə̀-chăng** (barefoot-wade-field)
foreign **wài-gwə-də** (outside-country-belonging)
foreigner **wài-gwə-rén** (outside-country-person)
forest **shù-lín-dz** (tree-forest)
forget **wàng-lə**: don't forget **byə́-wàng-lə**
forgive, pardon **ráu-shù**
fork **chā-dz**
form, shape **yàng-dz** (*also* sample, kind)
form into **dzàu-chə́ng** (build-convert)
Formosa **Tái-wăn**
fort **dyāu-bău** (bastion-castle)
fortification **güng-shìr** (work-job)
forty **sìr-shir** (four-ten)
forward **shyàng-chyán** (towards-front)
fountain **chyuán-shwŏi** (spring-water)
fountain pen **dzìr-lái-shwə́i-bĭ** (self-come-liquid-brush)
four **sìr**
fourth **dì-sìr-gə** (sequence-four-item), one fourth **sìr-fə̄n-dj yì** (four-division-derived one)
frame, rack, shelf **djyà-dz**
France **Fà-gwə**
free, having freedom **dzìr-yə́u**
free, gratis **myăn-fə̀i** (exempt-expense)
freeze, turn to ice **dùng-bìng-lə** (solidify-ice-done); freeze up, become solid **dùng-chi-lai** (solidify-up-come)
French **Fà-gwə-də** (France-belonging): French language **Fà-gwə-hwà** (France-words), Frenchman **Fà-gwə-rən** (France-person)
frequency **pín-lyù** (frequent-rate)
fresh **shin-shyan** (new-fresh)
friction **mwə́-tsā-lì** (grind-rub-force)

Friday **lǐ-bài-wǔ** (week-five)
friend **péng-yəu**
from **tsúng**: from here **tsúng-djə̀-li**, from now on **tsúng-shyàn-dzài-chǐ** (from-now-up)
front **chyán**: in front of the house **dzài-fáng-dz chyán-byan** (located-house front-side), go in front of the house **dàu-fáng-dz chyán-byan chyù** (reach-house front-side go), front wheel **chyán-lún**, battle front **chyán-shyàn** (front-line)
frost **shwǎng**
fruit **shwéi-gwǒ** (water-fruit)
fry **djyǎn**; fry in deep fat **djá**
fuel **rán-lyàu** (burn-stuff)
full **mǎn**
fur **máu** (*also* body-hair, wool)
furniture **djwə̄-yǐ** (table-chair)
fuse, circuit breaker **bǎu-shyǎn-sǐr** (protect-danger-strand); fuse for blasting **dàu-hwǒ-swə̄** (conduct-fire-cord)
fuselage **dji-shə̄n** (machine-body)
future, in the future **djyāng-lái** (will-come)

G

gage, meter, chart **byǎu** (*also* watch)
game, contest **yéu-shì** (mobile-drama)
garden **yuàn-dz**
garrison **djù-djyŭn** (reside-army)
gas, vapor, air **chì**: poison gas **dú-chì**, tear gas **tswə̄i-lèi dú-chì** (hurry-tears poison-gas)
gasket, washer **dyàn-chyuān** (pad-loop)
gasoline **chì-yéu** (gas-oil)
gas station **chì-yéu-djàn** (gas-oil-station)
gate **mén** (*also* door)
gather **shə̄u-djí** (gather-assemble)

gear-wheel **chǐr-lún** (tooth wheel)

general in the army **djyàng-gwan** (general-officer)

general store **dzǎ-hwə-pù** (sundry-goods-store) *or* **yáng-hwə-pù** (foreign-goods-store)

generally, usually **pǔ-tǔng** (*same as* common, ordinary): he generally lives in the city **tā pǔ-tǔng djù dzài-chéng-li** (him ordinary live located-city-in)

generator, dynamo **fā-dyàn-djî** (issue-electricity-machine)

gentlemen (*for addressing an audience*) **djū-wài** (all-respected)

geography **dì-lǐ** (land-arrange)

Germany **Dé-gwə**: German **Dé-gwə-də** (Germany-belonging), German language **Dé-gwə-hwà** (Germany-words), German person **Dé-gwə-rən** (Germany-person)

get, become **lə** (*tacked on-syllable*, done): get sick **bìng-lə** (sick-done), get well **hǎu-lə** (good-done), get soft **rwǎn-lə** (soft-done)

get, obtain **dé-dau** (obtain-reach); get, receive, accept **shōu-dàu** (collect-reach)

get away, escape **táu-lə**

get off **shyà** (*same as* down): get off a horse **shyà-mǎ** (down-horse), get off a vehicle **shyà-chə̄** (down-vehicle)

get on **shàng** (*same as* up): get on a horse **shàng-mǎ**

get up **chǐ-lai** (rise-come)

ghost **gwǒi**

gift **lǐ-wu** (polite-thing)

girl, young woman, Miss **shyǎu-djyə** (small-sister); girl child **nyǔ-hái-dz** (female-child)

give **gěi**

give up, surrender **tóu-shyáng** (bow-submit)

glad, happy **gāu-shìng** (high-spirits)

glass container **bēi-dz** (*same as* cup): a glass of water **yì-bēi shwǒi** (one-cup water) glass material, plate glass **bwě-li**

glasses, specs **yǎn-djing** (eye-lens); distance glasses, telescope **wàng-yuǎn-djìng** (gaze-far-lens)

glider **hwǎ-shyǎng-dji** (slide-soar-machine)

gloves **shǒu-tàu** (hand-sheath)

glue **djyǎu** (*sounds like* teach)

glycerin **gǎn-yǒu** (sweet-oil)

go **chyù**: go away **dzǒu-chyu** (leave-go), go back **hwéi-chyu** (return-go), go in **djìn-chyu** (enter-go), go out **chū-chyu** (exit-go)

go on, continue **djì-shyù**

goat, sheep **yáng** (*sounds like* ocean)

God **Shàng-dì** (Upper-emperor) *or* **Tyǎn-djǔ** (Heaven-master)

going to, shall, will **yàu** (*same as* want): it's going to rain **yàu shyà-yǔ** (want down-rain)

gold **djìn-dz**

good, satisfactory, O.K. **hǎu**: good-looking **hǎu-kàn** (good-look)

good-by, so long **dzài-djyàn** (again-see)

goods, merchandise **dūng-shi** (*same as* things) *or* **hwǒ-wu**

government **djàng-fǔ** (govern-residence)

governor **shěng-djǔ-shí** (state-chairman)

gown **cháng-shān** (long-robe); padded or lined gown **páu-dz**

grade, class, quality **děng**: first quality **yì-děng** (one-class)

grade in school **djí**: first grade in school **yì-djí** (one-grade)

grain **gǔ-dz**

gram **gūng-fēn** (universal-division): a gram of gold **yì-gūng-fēn djìn-dz** (one-gram gold)

grandchild **sūn-dz**

grandfather **dzǔ-fù**

grandmother **dzú-mǔ**

graphite **shír-mwǒ** (stone-ink)

grass **tsǎu** (*also* hay, straw)

grave, tomb **fén**

graveyard **fén-chǎng** (grave-field)

gravel **swèi-shír-təu** (broken-stone-head)

gray **hwǒi-də**

grease, oil **yéu**

great **dà** (*same as* big)

green, unripe **chǐng-də**

green-colored **lyù-də**

greeting **djǐng-lǐ** (*also* salute)

grenade (hand) **shǒu-lyéu-dàn** (hand-pomegranate-shell)

grind, sharpen **mwé**

grind up **mwè**

grindstone **shā-lún** (sand-wheel) *or* **mwè-dz**

grocery store **dzá-hwə-pù** (mixed-goods-shop)

groove, depression **tsáu**

ground, earth **dǐ** (*also* floor)

ground up **mwè-də** (grind-belonging)

group, herd **chyún**: a group of women **yǐ-chyún nyǚ-rən**
  (one-group woman)

grow **djǎng** *or* **djǎng-dà** (grow-big)

grown-up, adult **dà-rən** (big-person)

guarantee **bǎu-djèng** (protect-certificate)

guard, watchman, to guard **shǒu-wèi** (preserve-guard);
  military guard **wèi-bǐng** (guard-soldier)

guerrilla fighters **yéu-dji-dwèi** (mobile-strike-team)

guess **tsāi**

guest, visitor **kè-rən** (courtesy-person)

guide **lǐng-lù-də** (lead-road-belonging); to guide **lǐng-lù**
  (lead-road)

gully **gōu** (*also* ditch)

gun, small arm **chyǎng**; big gun, cannon **pàu**; grease gun
  yéu-chyǎng

gunpowder **hwǒ-yàu** (fire-medicine)
guts **cháng-dz**

H

habit, custom **shí-gwàn**
hacksaw **gāng-djyù** (steel-saw)
hair of body, wool **máu**; hair of head **tǒu-fa** (head-hair)
haircut **lǐ-fà** (arrange-hair)
half **bàn**: half of the butter **nyǒu-yǒu-də yí-bàn** (butter-belonging one-half), half a bowl of milk **bàn-wǎn nyǒu-nǎi** (half-bowl milk), half a month **bàn-gə yuǒ** (half-item month), half past three **sān-dyǎn-bàn** (three-mark-half)
hall for meetings **táng-dz**
hallway **gwǒ-dàur** (cross-way)
hammer **ding-chwǒi** (nail-hammer): sledge hammer **dà-chwǒi** (big-hammer), mallet **mù-chwǒi** (wood-hammer)
hand **shǒu**
hand over **dì-gəi** (transmit-give)
handcraft **shǒu-gūng-yǒ** (hand-industry)
handkerchief **shǒu-djyuàr** (hand-finecloth) *or* **shyáu-shǒu-djin** (small-towel)
handle, grip **bǐng** (*sounds like* cake) *or* **bàr**
hang up **gwà-chi-lai** (hang-up-come)
hangar **fǒi-dji-kù** (fly-machine-vault)
happen, take place **chū-shìr** (exit-matter): what happened? **chū shǒm-mə shìr** (exit what matter)
happen to **pòng-chyǎu** (*same as* accidentally): I happened to remember **wǒ pòng-chyǎu shyáng-chi-lai** (I accidentally remember)
happening, event **shìr-ching** (matter-fact)
happy **gāu-shìng** (high-spirits)
hard, firm **yìng**
hard to do, difficult **nán**

hard, energetically **shìr-djìn** (use-strength)

harbor **hǎi-kǒu** (sea-mouth)

harness **wǎn-djyù** (draw-gadget)

harvest, crops **djwǎng-djya** (farm-plants); to harvest **shǒu djwǎng-djya** (gather crops)

hat, cap **mǎu-dz**

hate, dislike **hèn**

have **yǒu**; haven't **méi-yǝu**

have to, must **yí-dìng yàu** (definitely will) *or* **děi**: I have to go **wǒ yí-dìng yàu-chyù** (I definitely will-go) *or* **wǒ děi-chyù** (I must-go)

he, him **tā** (*also* her, it)

head **tóu**: headache **tóu-téng**

head, chief **lǐng-shyǝu** (guide-sleeve); head officer **djǎng-gwān** (chief officer)

head (of livestock) **yì-pǐ** (one-head): three horses **sān-pǐ mǎ** (three-head horse)

headquarters **sìr-lìng-bù** (manage-orders-section)

healthy **shēn-ti hǎu** (body good): how's his health? **tā shēn-ti hǎu-bu-hǎu** (he body good-not-good)

hear **tīng-djyan** (listen-perceive): to hear it said **tīng-shwō** (hear-speak), I hear bells **wǒ tīng-djyan djüng** (I hear-perceive bell), I hear he's sick **wǒ tīng-shwō tā bìng-lǝ** (I hear-speak he sick)

heart **shīn** (*sounds like* new)

heat **rè** (*also* hot)

heavy **djùng** (*sounds like* cultivate, plant)

height **gāu-dù** (high-degree)

hello, how do you do **hǎu-bu-bǎu** (good-not-good) *or* **hǎu-a** (good-huh); hello (on telephone) **wǎi**; hello, hey! (calling attention) **ǎi**

helmet **gāng-kwēi** (steel-helmet)

help **bāng**: help me look for it **bāng-wǒ djǎu** (help-me seek), help him out **bāng-tā dzwò-shìr** (help-him do-work) help! **djyə̀u-mǐng** (save-life)

helper, assistant **djù-shǒu** (aid-hand)

her, she **tā** (*same as* him, it)

here **djə̀r** (used around Peiping) *or* **djə̀-li** (this-in): come here **dàu-djə̀-li lái** (reach-here come), he's here **tā dzài-djə̀-li** (he located-here)

hernia, rupture **shàn-chì**

hers **tā-də** (her-belonging)

hey! (calling attention) **ài**

hide, skin **pǐ**

hide, conceal **tsáng-chi-lai** (conceal-up-come): I hide **wǒ tsáng-chi-lai**, hide him **bǎ-tā tsáng-chi-lai** (take-him hide)

high, tall **gāu**: high pressure, high tension **gāu-yā** (high-press), high test gas **gāu-dù chǐ-yǒu** (high-degree gasoline)

high-priced, expensive **gwə̀i**

highway **gūng-lù** (public-road)

hill, mountain **shān**

him, he **tā** (*same as* her, it)

hinge **hə́-yə̀** (together-leaf)

hire **gù**

his, hers, its **tā-də** (him-belonging)

history **lì-shǐr**

hit, beat, whip **dǎ**; hit the mark **dǎ-djùng** (hit-spot)

hoe **chú-təu** (hoe-head)

hold, take hold **bǎ**

hold back, hold-off **lyə́u-shyà** (retain-down)

hole, tunnel **dùng** (*sounds like* move); hole, vent (in machinery) **mə́n** (*same as* door)

hollow **kǔng-shǐn** (empty-heart)

home **djyā** (*also* family): at home **dzài-djyā-li** (located-home-in)

honest **lǎu-shir** (honesty-solid)

honorable **gwə̀i** (*also* expensive), *used in polite conversation*: what is your name? **gwə̀i-shìng** (honorable-surname), my

name's Li **bĭ-shĭng Lĭ** (humble-surname Li), what country? **gwəi-gwə́** (honorable-country), my country is Texas
bĭ-gwə́ shĭr Texas (humble-country be Texas)

hook **gə̄u-dz**

hook on **gə̄u-shang** (hook-on): hook it on **bǎ-ta gə̄u-shang**
(take-it hook-on)

hope for **shĭ-wǎng**: we hope that you will come **wə̆-mən
shĭ-wǎng nĭ lái** (we hope you come)

horizon **shwə̆i-píng-shyàn** (water-level-line) *or* **dĭ-píng-
shyàn** (land-level-line)

horizontal **píng-də** (*also* smooth) *or* **hə́ng-də**

horse **mǎ**: one-horsepower **yĭ-pi mǎ-lĭ** (one-head horse-
power)

horseshoe **mǎ-tí-tyə̆** (horse-hoof-iron)

hose, water pipe **shwə́i-gwǎn-dz** (water-tube)

hospital **yĭ-yuàn** (cure-court)

host, person in charge **djŭ-rən** (master-person)

hot, warm **rə̀**; pepper-hot **là** (*sounds like* wax)

hotel **fàn-dyàn** (food-shop) *or* **lyú-gwǎn** (travel-establish-
ment)

hour **djŭng-tə́u** (clock-end): an hour **yĭ-gə djŭng-tə́u** (one-
item hour)

house **fáng-dz**

how? in what way? **dzə̆m-mə-yàng** (how-manner); how are
you? **nĭ hǎu-bu-hǎu** (you good-not-good) *or* **nĭ hǎu-ma**
(you good-huh); how come? why? **wəi-shə́m-mə** (because-
what)

how about? **nə** (*tacked on syllable*): how about you? **nĭ-nə**
(you-howabout)

how much, how many **dwə̄-shau** (much-little); how big?
dwə̄-dà (much-big); how far? **dwə̄-yuǎn** (much-far)

humble **bĭ** (*see examples under* honorable)

hundred **bǎi**: a hundred men **yĭ-bǎi rə́n** (one-hundred person)

hungry **yằu-chìr** (want-eat) *or* **ə**: I'm hungry **wŏ yằu-chìr**
(I want-eat) *or* **wŏ hĕn-ə** (I very-hungry)

hunt for, look for **djău**

hunt game **dă** (*same as* hit) *or* **dă-lyə** (hit-hunt): he hunted
deer **tā dă-lù** (him hit-deer), he goes hunting **tā chyù
dă-lyə** (he go hit-hunt)

hurry, in a hurry **tsūng-máng** (hurry-busy)

hurt, injury **shāng**; get hurt, get wounded **shəu-shāng**
(receive injury)

hurts, is painful **téng**

husband **djằng-fu** (tenfeet-fellow) *or* **shyăn-shəng** (*same as*
Mister)

I

I, me **wŏ**

ice **bīng** (*sounds like* soldier)

idea, opinion **yì-djyan** (mind-perceive)

ideals **lĭ-shyăng** (principle-thought)

if **yằu-shìr** (want-be, *always used with* then): give it to him
if he wants it **yằu-shìr tā yằu nĭ djyəu gŏi-ta** (if he want,
you then give-him)

ignition **dyàn-hwŏ** (electric-fire)

ill, illness **bìng**

imitate **mwŏ-făng**

imitation **făng-dzằu-də** (imitate-construct-belonging)

immediately **yí-kàn djyəu** (one-look then): he went immediately **tā yí-kàn djyəu chyù** (he one-look then go)

important **yằu-djìn**

in **lĭ** (*used with* located) *or* **djìn** (*same as* enter): in the house
dzài-fáng-dz-li (located-house-in), go in **djìn-chyu** (enter-
go), come in **djìn-lai** (enter-come)

inch **yīng-tsùn** (English-shortmeasure), *but centimeters*
(**gūng-fən**) *are in more general use*

including **bău-kwə** (wrap-include)

increase **djyǎ-dwǒ** (add-much) *or* **djǎng** (*same as* grow)

India **Yìn-du**

Indo-China, Annam **Ǎn-nán** (Peace-south)

Indo-Chinese **Ǎn-nán-də** (Annam-belonging): Indo-Chinese language **Ǎn-nán-hwà** (Annam-words), Indo-Chinese person **Ǎn-nán-rən** (Annam-person)

industry **gūng-yə̀** (work-industry): heavy industry **djùng gūng-yə̀**, light industry **chīng gūng-yə̀**, textile industry **fǎng-djǐr gūng-yə̀** (spin-weave industry), hand industries **shǒu gūng-yə̀**, mining industry **kwàng-yə̀** (mine-industry)

infantry, infantryman **bù-bīng** (step-soldier)

infected **hǎi-chi-lai** (infect-up-come)

infection **fā-yán** (issue-inflammation)

inform, tell about **gǎu-sung** *or* **gǎu-su**

information **chǐng-bǎu** (fact-report)

inhale, draw in **chə̄u** (*same as* suck) *or* **shǐr**

inherit **chéng-dji**

ink **mwə̀-shwǒi** (ink-water)

insect **chúng-dz**

insignia **hwə̀i-djǎng**

inspection, censorship, to inspect **djyǎn-chá** (examine-investigate)

installments, to pay in installments **fə̄n-chī fù-kwǎn** (part pay-debt)

instead of **tì**: go instead of me **tì-wǒ chyu** (instead-me go)

instructions **djǐr-shǐr** (point-reveal)

instruments **yǐ-chǐ** (apparatus-device)

insulation, to insulate **djyuə́-yuán** (block-connection)

insurance, to insure **bǎu-shyǎn** (protect-danger)

interest (on a loan) **lì-chyán** (interest-money)

interesting **yǒu-yì-sir** (have-meaning)

interpret, translate **fǎn-yi**

interpreter **fǎn-yi-yuán** (translate-personnel)

introduce (people) **djyə-shàu**: letter of introduction **djyə-shàu-shìn** (introduce-letter)

invite **chǐng** (*also* request, please): I invite you to eat **wǒ chíng-nǐ chǐr-fàn** (I invite-you eat-food)

iodine tincture **dyán-djyǒu** (iodine-wine)

iron **tyǒ**: iron foundry **tyǒ-gūng-chǎng** (iron-factory)

is, am, are **shìr** (*more information under* be)

island **dǎu**

issue, give out **fā**

itch **yǎng**: to itch **fā-yǎng** (issue-itch)

J

jack for lifting **chyān-djìn** (thousand-pounds)

jacket, coat **gwà-dz**

jail, prison **djyān-yù**

jam, jelly **táng-djyàng** (candy-paste)

Japan **Rìr-bǒn** (sun-origin)

Japanese **Rìr-bǒn-də** (Japan-belonging): Japanese language **Rìr-bǒn-hwà** (Japan-words), Japanese person **Rìr-bǒn-rén** (Japan-person)

jar (large), pot **hú** (*sounds like* lake); small jar, can (for preserves) **gwàn**: a jar of fruit **yí-gwàn shwěi-gwǒ** (one-container fruit)

jeep **djí-pu-chə** (jeep-vehicle)

Jesus **Yə-sū**

job, work, business **shìr** (*sounds like* be)

join a group **djyā-rù**: will you join us? **nǐ djyā-rù bù-djyā-rù wǒ-mən** (you join not-join us)

join ends, make a joint **djyə-chi-lai** (receive-up-come)

joke **shyàu-hwa** (laugh-words)

juice **djìr**

jump **tyàu**

just, exactly **gǎng-gǎng**: just right **gǎng-hǎu** (just-good),
just six o'clock **djǔn-lyǝu-dyǎn** (exact-six-mark), just
eight years old **gǎng-gǎng bā-swǝi**, just now **gǎng-tsái**

K

keep in a condition **bǎu-chír**: keep this thing clean **djǝ-gǝ
yúng-yuǎn yí-dǐng-yǎu gān-djǐng á** (this always definitely-
will clean, huh?)
keep in a place **fàng** (*same as* put): keep it in the basket
bǎ-ta fàng dzài-lán-dz-li (take-it put located-basket-in)
kettle **shwǝi-hú** (water-pot)
key **yǎu-shir**
khaki, tan **kǎ-dji-bù-sǝ-dǝ** (khaki-cloth-color-belonging)
kick **tī**
kill with a weapon **shā-sǐr** (slay-dead); kill by striking
dá-sǐr (hit-dead)
kilocycle **chyǎn-djǝu-bwǝ** (thousand-period-wave)
kilogram **gǔng-djǐn** (universal-weightunit)
kilometer **gǔng-lǐ** (universal-mile): a kilometer **yǐ-gǔng-li**
(one-kilometer)
kilowatt **chyǎn-wǎ** (thousand-watt)
kind, species **djǔng**: this kind **djǝ-djǔng**, one kind **yǐ-djǔng**
kind-hearted **tsír-shàn**
king **gwǝ-wáng** (country-king)
kiss **chīn-chin**
kitchen **chú-fáng** (cook-house)
Korea **gāu-li**
Korean **gāu-li-dǝ** (Korea-belonging): Korean language
Gāu-li-hwà (Korea-words), Korean person **Gāu-li-rǝn**
(Korea-person)
knee **shǐ-gài** (knee-cover)
knife **dāu-dz** (*also* blade)
knock at the door **dǎ-mǝn** (hit-door)

knock down **dǎ-shyà** (hit-down)

knot (in rope) **djyə̌**; to tie a knot **djyə̌-chi-lai** (knot-up-come)

know (something) **djìr-dau**; know (people) **rə̀n-shir**; know how **hwə̀i**: I know that **wǒ djìr-dau nà-gə**, he knows me **tā rə̀n-shir wǒ**, he knows English **tā hwə̀i-shwə̄ Yǐng-gwə-hwà** (he knowhow-speak English)

Kuomintang **Gwə̌-mín-dǎng** (Country-people-party)

L

label **byǎu-chyǎn** (mark-slip)

ladder **tǐ-dz**

ladle, dipper **shǎu-dz**

lake **hú** (*sounds like* small pot)

lamb **shyǎu-yáng** (small-sheep): lamb meat **yáng-rə̀u** (sheep-meat)

lamp, light **də̄ng**

land, soil **dì**

land, come to land (from air) **djyàng-là**; to land (from water) **də̄ng-lù** (mount-dryland)

landmark **byǎu-djìr** (mark-remember)

language **hwà** (*same as* words) *or* **wə́n**: English language **yǐng-gwə-hwà** (English-country-words) *or* **yǐng-wə́n** (English-language), Chinese language **djǔng-gwə-hwà** *or* **djǔng-wə́n**

lard **djǔ-yə́u** (pig-grease)

last before now **shàng** (*sounds like* on, up): last month **shàng-yuə̀**, last time **shàng-tsìr**, last two times **shàng-lyǎng-tsìr**; last year **chyù-nyan** (go-year); last of all **dzwə̀i-hə̀u** (most-behind): the last one to come **dzwə̀i-hə̀u-lái-də yí-gə rən** (most-behind-come-belonging one person)

latch **shwǎn-dz**

late **wǎn-lə**: he came late **tā lái wǎn-lə**, it's late now **shyàn-dzài wǎn-lə** (now late)

later on **hòu-lái** (behind-come)

latrine, toilet **tsò-swǒ** (latrine-structure)

laugh, smile **shyàu**: laugh out loud **dà-shyàu** (big-laugh)

launder **shǐ-yī** (wash-clothes), launderer **shǐ-yī-də** (wash-clothes-belonging)

laundry **shǐ-yī-dyàn** (wash-clothes-shop) *or* **shǐ-yī-fáng** (wash-clothes-house)

law **fǎ-lyù** (rule-statute)

lawyer **lyù-shîr** (statute-scholar)

laxative **shyò-yàu** (diarrhea-medicine)

lay an egg **shyà-dàn** (down-egg)

lay down **fàng** (*same as* put)

layer **tséng**: a layer of straw **yì-tséng tsǎu** (one-layer straw)

lazy **lǎn**

lead (metal) **chyān** (*sounds like* thousand)

lead, take along **dài**; lead, guide to **lǐng-dàu** (guide-reach); lead, serve as leader **lǐng-dǎu** (guide-conduct): he led the horse **tā dài-mǎ chyu** (he lead-horse go), he led the people to the house **tā lǐng-rén dàu-fáng-dz nà-li chyu** (he guide-person reach-house there go), he led his soldiers very well **tā-lǐng-dǎu-bīng lǐng-dǎu-də hén-hǎu** (he-guide-conduct-soldier guide-conduct-belonging very-good)

leader, chief **lǐng-shyòu** (guide-sleeve)

leaf **yò** (*sounds like* night)

leaflet **chwán-dān** (transmit-bill)

leak, seep out **lòu**: the pot leaks **hú lòu-shwǒi** (pot leak-water)

learn, study **shyué**

leather **pí-dz**

leave, go away **dzǒu** (*also* walk); leave alone **fàng-shǒu** (put-hand); leave behind **lyóu-shya-lə** (remain-down-done): he left the house **tā tsúng-fáng-dz dzǒu chyù** (he from-house leave-go), leave that man alone **bǎ-nà-gə-rən fàng-shǒu** (take-that-person put-hand), I left your hat **wǒ lyǒu-shya-lə nǐ-də màu-dz** (I remain-down-done you-belonging hat)

leave of absence, on vacation **fàng-djyà-lə** (put-vacation-done)

left side **dzwǒ-byan**: on the left **dzài-dzwǒ-byan** (located-left-side)

leg **twǒi**

lemon **níng-mǒng** (*supposed to sound like English*)

lend **djyə̀-gəi** (loan-give)

length **cháng-dù** (long-degree)

lens **tə̀u-djìng** (thru-mirror)

leprosy **má-fə̄ng**

less **shǎu** (*same as* little, *used with* compare): I have less money than he **wǒ-də chyán bǐ-tā shǎu** (me-belonging money compare-him little); less so **mǒi nə̀-mə** (haven't thus): he's less clever than you **tā mǒi-nǐ nə̀-mə tsūng-ming** (he haven't-you thus clever)

lesson **gūng-kə̀**; one lesson **yí-kə̀**

let, permit **ràng**: let him do it **ràng-tā dzwə̀** (permit-him do)

let go, release **fàng-lə** (put-done); leggo! **fàng-shǒu** (put-hand)

letter, message **shìn**

letter of the alphabet **dzìr-mǔ** (wordsign-mother)

level, flat, smooth **píng-də**; spirit level **shwǒi-píng-chì** (water-level-device)

library **tú-shū-gwǎn** (picture-book-establishment)

lice **shir-dz** (*sounds like* lion)

lie, speak untruth **shwə̄-hwǎng** (speak-lie)

lie down **tǎng-shya** (recline-down); lying on **tǎng-dzài** (recline-located) lieutenant (first) **djŭng-wði** (middle-companyofficer), second lieutenant **shðu-wði** (junior-companyofficer)

life, existence **shə̄ng-hwə** (born-alive): I've lived here all my life **wš yì-djír dzði-djə̀-li djù** (I one-straight located-here reside)

lift (small thing) **ná-chi-lai** (pickup-up-come); lift (large thing), raise bodily **tái-chi-lai;** lift, pull up (by a handle) **tí-chi-lai**

light, lamp **də̄ng;** light for a cigarette **hwš** (*same as* fire): lights in general **də̄ng-hwš** (lamp-fire)

light up, kindle **dyǎn** (*sounds like* point)

light-colored **chyǎn**

light, not dark **lyàng:** it's still light **tyǎn hái-lyàng** (sky still-light)

lighten **dá-shǎn** (hit-lightning)

lightning **shǎn-dyàn** (lightning-electric)

lightweight **ching**

like, care for **shǐ-hwan**

like, resembling **shyàng** (*sounds like* towards): I am like you **wš shyàng nǐ** (I resemble you)

lime (calcium oxide) **shír-hwə̄i** (stone-ash)

line **shyàn** (*also* thread, wire)

line of battle **djàn-shyàn** (fight-line)

liquid **yə̀-tǐ** (liquid-body) *or* **shwši** (*same as* water)

liquor **djyšu** (*same as* wine)

list **dān-dz:** name list, roster **míng-dān**

listen, listen to **tīng:** listen to me **tīng-wš**

literature **wš́n-shyuš́** (literature-study)

litter, stretcher **dān-djyà** (yoke-frame)

little, small **shyǎu;** little, not much **shǎu;** a little bit **yǐ-dyǎr** *or* **yì-dyǎn** (one-mark)

live, reside, stop over **djù:** I live here **wš dzài-djə̀-li djù** (I located-here reside) livestock **shəng-kŏu** (creature-mouth)

living, alive **hwə́-dj** (alive-remain)

load (gun) **djwăng dzĭr-dăn** (load cartridge); load (vehicle) **djwăng-hwə̀** (load-goods); one load **yĭ-chə̄** (one-vehicle): a load of hay **yĭ-chə̄ tsău** (one-vehicle hay)

loan **djyə̀-kwăn** (borrow-debt); to loan, lend **djyə̀-gəi** (loan-give)

lock, padlock **swŏ**; to lock up **swŏ-chi-lai** (lock-up-come)

lockjaw **pwə̀-shăng-fə̄ng** (break-injury-wind)

locomotive **hwŏ-chə̄-tə́u** (fire-vehicle-head)

log **dă-mù-təu** (big-wood-head)

long **cháng** (*sounds like* taste): long in duration **cháng-djyŏu** (long-lasting), the rope is very long **shə́ng-dz hŏn-cháng** (rope very-long), how long a time? **dwə̄-djyŏu**, long time no see **háu-djyŏu bú-djyàn** (good-longtime not-see)

look, look at, watch **kàn** (*also* visit)

look for, seek **djău**

looking glass **djìng-dz**

loom **djir-bù-djī** (weave-cloth-machine)

loop **chyuăr** *or* **chyuăn-dz**

loose **sŭng**

lose, mislay **dyə̄u-lə**; lose a battle **dă-băi-lə** (hit-defeat-done); lose in a game **shŭ-lə**; lose time **fə̀i-shír-həu** (spend-time); lose money (in business) **pə́i-chyán** (compensate-money); lose face **dyə̄u-lyăn**

losses **sŭn-shîr** (damage-loss)

loud **dă-shə̄ng** (big-voice): speak loud **dă-shə̄ng shwə̀-hwà** (big-voice speak-words)

louse **shîr-dz** (*sounds like* lion)

love **shǐ-hwan** (*same as* like) *or* **ài**

low **dī**

lower, let down **shyà** (*also* down)

lubricate **djyā hwá-yə́u** (add slide-oil)

lucky **shìng-yùn** (blessed-fate); good luck on the road **yí-lù píng-ǎn** (one-road safe); good luck in your work **djú-nǐ chéng-gūng** (pray-you succeed-work)

lumber **mù-lyàu** (wood-stuff)

lump, hunk, piece **kwài**: a lump **yí-kwài** (one-piece)

lungs **fèi**

M

machine **dji-chi** (machine-device)

machine-gun **djî-gwǎn-chyǎng** (machine-shut-smallarm)

machine shop **djî-chi-chǎng** (machine-device-factory)

magnet **tsír-tyǒ** (magnetism-iron); electro-magnet **dyàn-tsír-tyǒ**; magnetic north **tsír-djèn-běi** (magnetism-pin-north)

maid **lǎu-mǎ-dz** (old-servantwoman)

mail **shìn** (*same as* letters); to mail letters **djì-shìn**

main, principal **djǔ-yàu-də** (master-want-belonging) *or* **dà** (*same as* big): main force **djǔ-lì** (master-power), main road **dà-lù** (big-road), main gate **dà-mén** (big-gate)

mainland **dà-lù** (big-mainland, *sounds like* big-road)

major (army) **shàu-shyàu** (junior-fieldgrade)

make, do **dzwò** (*sounds like* sit); make, build **dzàu** (*also* to manufacture); make to do **djyàu** (*also* tell to do); make so **nùng**: he made this hat **tā dzwò djè-gə màu-dz** (he make this hat), he made a house **tā dzàu fáng-dz** (he build house), he made me fall **tā djyàu-wǒ shwāi-dǎu-lə** (he order-me fall-down), make this clean **bǎ-djè-gə nùng-gān-djing-lə** (take-this make-clean-done)

malaria **yàu-dz** (in North China) *or* **bǎi-dz** (in South China); have malaria **fā-yàu-dz** (issue-malaria) *or* **dá-bǎi-dz** (hit malaria)

Malay **Mǎ-lái**

male (animal) **gūng-də**; male (person) **nán-də**

man, person **rə́n**; man, male person **nán-rən** (male-person)

manage, be in charge of **gwǎn**; manage (a business), manager **djing-lǐ** (transact-manage)

manners, courtesy **lǐ-màu**

manpower **rə́n-lǐ** (person-power)

manufacture **dzàu** (*also* build)

manure, dung **shǐr**

many, much **dwə̄**

map **dì-tú** (land-picture); road map **lù-shyàn-tú** (road-line-picture)

mark **djì-hau** (copy-sign); distinguishing mark, emblem **hwə̀i-djǎng**

market **shǐr-chǎng** (market-field)

married, to marry **djyə́-hūn-lə** (knit-marriage-done)

mask **djyǎ-myàn-djyù** (false-face-gadget)

mat **shí-dz**

mate with, match with **pə̀i**

matches **yáng-hwə̌** (overseas-fire)

materials **gūng-lyàu** (work-stuff); raw materials **yuán-lyàu** (original-stuff)

matter, job, work **shǐr** (*sounds like* be); matter, affair, circumstance **shǐr-ching**

mattress **rù-dz**

maximum **dzwə̀i-dà** (most-big)

may, allowed to **kə́-yi** (*also* maybe): you may go there **nǐ kə́-yi dàu-nà-li chyu** (you allowed reach-there go)

maybe **kə́-yi** (*also* allowed); it may happen **kə́-yi chū-shǐr** (maybe exit-event)

mayor **tsūn-djǎng** (village-chief) *or* **chə́ng-djǎng** (city-chief)

me, I **wə̌**

meal, food **fàn**

meal, ground grain **fə̌n** (*same as* powder)

meaning **yì-sir**

measuring device **lyáng-chĭ**; to measure **lyáng**

meat **ròu**

mechanic **dji-gūng** (machine-work)

medical science **yĭ-shyuǒ** (heal-study); medical school **yĭ-shuǒ-shyàu**; medical officer **yĭ-gwān** (heal-officer)

medicines **yàu** (*sounds like* want)

medium-sized **djūng-hàur-də**; medium-quality **djūng-djungr-də** (middle-middling-belonging)

meet **pèng-djyan** (collide-see)

meeting **hwèi**; hold a meeting **kāi-hwèi** (open-meet)

melon **gwā**; watermelon **shi-gwa** (west-melon)

melt **rúng-hwà-lə** (dissolve-transform-done)

member (of a group) **hwèi-yuán** (organization-personnel)

mend, patch up **bŭ-yi-bu** (mend-one-mend)

merchant **mǎi-mai-rən** (buy-sell-person) *or* **shāng-rən** (commerce-person)

message, letter **shìn**; word-of-mouth message **shyǎu-shi**

messenger **sùng-shìn-də** (send-letter-belonging)

metal **djin-shŭ** (gold-group)

meter, gage **byǎu** (*also* clock *and* chart)

meter (39.37 inches) **gūng-chĭr** (universal-lengthunit): one meter **yĭ-gūng-chĭr**

method **fá-dz**

microphone **sùng-hwà-chĭ** (send-words-device)

middle **djūng-djyǎn** (middle-space)

midnight **bàn-yè** (half-night)

midwife **shōu-shēng-də** (collect-born-belonging)

might, maybe **kǒ-yi** (*also* allowed): it might rain **kǒ-yi shyà-yŭ** (maybe down-rain)

mile **ying-lĭ** (English-mile); Chinese mile (about half a kilometer) **lĭ**; *the official unit is the* kilometer **gūng-lĭ** (universal-mile)

military **djyūn** (*same as* army): military uniform **djyūn-yi** (army-clothing), military personnel **djyŭn-rən** (army-person), military government **djyŭn-djàng-fŭ**

milk **năi**: cow's milk **nyóu-năi**

million **yì-băi-wàn** (one-hundred-tenthousand)

mine, my **wǒ-də** (me-belonging)

mine (explosive) **dì-lói** (land-thunder)

mine for minerals **kwàng** (*also* ore): coal mine **mói-kwàng**, iron mine **tyǒ-kwàng** (*also* iron-ore)

minerals **kwàng-wu** (ore-thing)

minimum **dzwèi-shyău** (most-small)

minister, head of a government department **bù-djăng** (section-head)

minister, priest **djyàu-shir** (teaching-person)

minus **djyăn** (*same as* subtract): five minus three is two **wŭ djyăn-săn shìr-àr** (five subtract-three be-two)

minute **fèn-djŭng** (division-clock): please wait a minute **chíng-dèng yì-fèn-djŭng** (request-wait one-division-clock)

mirror **djìng-dz**

Miss, young lady **shyău-djyə** (small-sister): Miss Li **Lǐ-shyău-djyə** (Li-Miss)

miss, fail to hit **dǎ-bŭ-djùng** (strike-not-hit); missed **mói-yəu dǎ-djùng** (haven't strike-hit)

missing, lacking, to disappear **bú-djyàn-lə** (not-perceive-done)

mission, purpose **dzŭng-djìr** (main-theme)

mission (religious) **chwán-djyàu** (spread-teaching, *sounds like* boat-teaching)

missionary **chwán-dàu-də** (spread-reach-belonging)

missionize **chwán-dàu** (spread-reach)

mist **wù** (*also* fog)

mistake **tswò-wu**; to make a mistake **tswò-lə** (mistake-done): he made a mistake in writing **tā shyǒ-tswò-lə** (he write-mistake-done)

Mister, gentlemen **shyăn-shəng** (first-born, *same as* husband, teacher): Mister Li **Lĭ-shyan-shəng** (Li-Mister)

mix together **hùn-chi-lai** (mix-up-come)

mixed, assorted **shír-djĭn-də** (ten-variety-belonging)

mixture **hùn-hə́-wù** (mix-together-thing)

model, pattern **yăng-shir** (shape-form)

Mohammedanism **Hwə́i-djyàu** (Mohammedan-teaching); a
Mohammedan person **Hwə́i-hwəi**

momentum **dùng-lyăng** (move-quantity)

Monday **lĭ-băi-yĭ** (week-one)

money **chyán**

Mongolia **Mə̆ng-gu**; Mongolian language **Mə̆ng-gu-hwă**
(Mongolia-words); Mongol **Mə̆ng-gu-rən** (Mongolia-per-
son)

month **yuə̀** (*also* moon): a month **yí-gə yuə̀** (one-item
month), month of January **yĭ-yuə** (One-month), Month
of December **shír-ə̀r-yuə** (Twelve-month)

more so **yĭ-dyăr** (*same as* one-bit): more **dwə̀-yi-dyar**
(much-one-bit), more slowly **măn-yi-dyar** (slow-one-bit)

morning **dzău-shang** (early-up)

morphine **mă-fə̀i** (*like English*)

mosquito **wə́n-dz**: mosquito bar **wə́n-djàng** (mosquito-
canopy)

most of all **dzwə̀i**: most in amount **dzwə̀i-dwə̄** (most-much),
highest **dzwə̀i-gāu** (most-high), most of them, the majority **dà-dwə̄-shù** (big-much-number)

mother **mŭ-chin**

motor, engine **fā-dùng-dji** (issue-motion-machine) *or* **dji-chĭ**
(*same as* machine)

motorcycle **ə̀r-lún-kă** (two-wheel-car)

mount (horse) **chí-shang** (straddle-up)

mountain **shān** (*same as* hill) *or* **dà-shān** (big-hill): mountain range **shān-măi** (mountain-veins)

mouse **hàu-dz** (*also* rat)

mouth **dzwǒi**; river mouth **hǒ-kǒu**

movable **nǎng-dùng-də** (able-move-belonging)

move (change one's location) **dùng**: don't move **byǒ-dùng**

move (a thing) **bǎn**

movie **dyàn-yǐng** (electric-shadow): movie theater **dyàn-yǐng-yuàn** (electric-shadow-court)

Mr., gentleman **shyān-shəng** (first-born, *same as* husband, teacher): Mr. Li **Lǐ-Shyan-shəng** (Li-Mister)

Mrs., lady, married woman **tài-tai**: Mrs. Li **Lǐ-Tai-tai** (Li-Mrs.)

much, many **dwǒ**

mud **ní** (*sounds like* wool cloth)

muffler, silencer **shyāu-shǒng-chǐ** (lessen-noise-device)

mule **lwǒ-dz**

museum **bwǒ - wù - gwǎn** (comprehensive - thing - establishment); art museum **yǐ-shù-gwǎn** (art-craft-establish-dzǒu (me ment)

music **yīn-yuǒ** (sound-music)

must **yǐ-dìng yǎu** (definitely will) *or* **dǒi**: I must go **wǒ yǐ-dìng yǎu-dzǒu** (me definitely will leave) *or* **wǒ dǒi-dzǒu**

mutiny **bīng-byàn** (soldier-mutiny)

muzzle **pàu-kǒu** (cannon-mouth) *or* **chyǎng-kǒu** (smallarm-mouth)

my, mine **wǒ-də** (me-belonging)

N

nail, spike **dìng-dz**

name **míng-dz**; family name, surname **shìng**; full name **shìng-míng** (surname-name)

narrow **djǎi**

natural, genuine **tyān-rán-də** (nature-like-belonging)
naturally, of course **dāng-rán** (right-like)
navy **hǎi-djyūn** (sea-army)
near, vicinity **fù-djìn** (attached-near): in the neighborhood
  dzài-fù-djìn (located-near), near the house **dzài-fáng-dz
  fù-djìn** (located-house near)
necessary, to need **shyū-yàu** (must-want)
necktie **lǐng-dài** (neck-belt)
negative film **dǐ-pyàn** (bottom-card)
negative terminal **yin-djí** (negative-extremity)
needle **djən** (*also* pin)
neighbor **lín-djyu** (neighboring-dwell)
nerve **shén-djing** (spirit-fiber)
nervous, excited **hwǎng-lə**
net **wǎng**
neutral country **djūng-lì-gwá** (middle-stand-country)
never yet **méi-yǒu-gwə** (haven't-cross), never will **yǔng-bū**
  (forever-not): he's never spoken **tā méi-yǒu shwá-gwə**
  (he haven't speak-cross), I'll never smoke **wǒ yǔng bù-
  chəu-yān** (I forever not-suck-tobacco)
new **shin-də**
news (published or broadcast) **shin-wén** (new-hear); word-
  of-mouth news **shyāu-shi**
newspaper **bàu**
next **shyà** (*also* down): the next one **shyà-yi-gə**, next
  month **shyà-yuə**, next time **shyà-tsìr**, next two times
  shyà-lyǎng-tsìr; next year **míng-nyan** (morrow-year)
nice, good **hǎu**
nighttime **yə-li** (night-in); a night **yǐ-tyān wǎn-shang** (one-
  day late-on)
nine **djyǒu** (*sounds like* wine)
ninety **dyjǒu-shir** (nine-ten)

ninth **dǐ-djyǒu-gə** (sequence-nine-item); one ninth **djyǒu-fən-dj yǐ** (nine-division-derived one)

no **bū** (*same as* not, *always used with some other word*): no, it's not so **bú-shǐr** (not-be), no, it's not good **bù-hǎu** (not-good), no, I don't want to **wǒ bú-yàu** (I not-want)

no, none **méi-yǒu** (*same as* haven't): I have no money **wǒ méi-yəu chyán** (I haven't money), there is no meat **méi-yəu ròu** (haven't meat)

nobody **méi-rən** *or* **méi-yəu-rən** (haven't person): nobody came **méi-rən lái**

noise, sounds **shəng-yin**

noisy **nàu**

noodles **myàn-tyáu** (flour-strip)

noon **djūng-wǔ** (middle-noon)

north **bǒi**: in the north **dzài-bǒi-byan** (located-north-side), go north **shyàng-bǒi-byan chyù** (towards-north-side go), northern part of China **djüng-gwə-də bǒi-bù** (China-belonging north-section), north star **bǒi-djí-shing** (north-extremity-star)

nose **bí-dz**

not **bū**: it's not good **bù-hǎu**, it's not here **bú-shǐr dzài-djə-li** (not-be located-here), I do not want it **wǒ bú-yàu-ta** (I not-want-it)

notebook, pad of paper **djír-bǒn-dz** (paper-volume)

notes (jotted down) **bǐ-djì** (brush-record)

nothing **shə́m-mə dəu bū** *or* **méi-yəu** (what all not *or* haven't): nothing is good **shə́m-mə dəu-bù-hǎu** (what all-not-good), there's nothing **shə́m-mə dəu méi-yǒu** (what all haven't)

notice (announcement), to notice **djù-yì** (inject-idea)

now **shyàn-dzài** (present-located)

nozzle **lúng-tə́u** (dragon-head)

number, amount **shù-mu**

number one **yi-hàu** (one-numbered): room number six
lyàu-hàu fáng-djyán (six-numbered house-space), sixth of
May **wǔ-yuà lyàu-hàu** (Five-month six-numbered)
nurse, look after **kǎn-hu** (watch-protect)
nut for a bolt **lwǒ-sir-màu** (bolt-hat)
nuts **gǎn-gwǒ-dz** (dry-fruit)

O

oar **djyǎng** (*also* paddle)
obey **tìng** (*same as* listen): obey him **tìng tǎ-də hwà** (listen
him-belonging words)
oblique **shyǒ-də**
observe **gwǎn-chá** (observe-estimate)
obstacle **djàng-ài**
ocean **yáng** (*sounds like* goat, sheep)
o'clock **dyǎn-djüng** (mark-clock): one o'clock **yì-dyǎn-djung**
of **də** (*tacked on syllable*, belonging); she's the wife of a
soldier **tǎ shìr yí-gə-bìng-də tài-tai** (her be one-soldier-
belonging wife)
off **shyà** (*same as* down): he got off the train **tǎ shyà-hwǒ-
chə** (he down-train)
offer **gùng-shyàn** (supply-present)
office **bàn-gùng-shìr** (handle-work-chamber)
officer, official **gwǎn**: army officer **djyǔn-gwǎn**, official language **gwǎn-hwà** (officer-words)
officer, policeman **djǐng-chá** (lookout-inspector)
often **cháng-cháng**
ohm **əu-mu** (*like English*)
oil, grease **yǒu**: engine oil **dji-chì-yǒu**, oil well **yǒu-djǐng**
old, not new **djyòu** (*sounds like* then); old, not young **lǎu**;
old-style, old-fashioned **lǎu-shìr-də** (old-affair-belonging)
old, years of age **swèi**: how old is he? **tǎ djǐ-swèi** (he

howmany-ageyear), ten years old **shír-swòi** (ten-age year), the car is two years old **chǐ-chǝ̄ shìr chyán lyǎng-nyán-dǝ** (gas-cart be before two-year-belonging)

on, get on **shàng** (*also* up): on the hill **dzài-shān-shang** (located-hill-on), onto the hill **dǎu-shān-shang** (reach-hill-on), he got on a horse **tā shàng-mǎ** (he up-horse), get on the wagon **shàng-chǝ̄** (up-vehicle)

once **yí-tsìr** (one-time)

once upon a time **yǒu-yì-tyān** (have-one-day)

one **yì** (*used with tacked-on classifiers*): one-item person **yí-gǝ rǝ́n** (item *for persons and things not covered by other classifiers*), one-strip road **yì-tyáu lù** (strip *for belts, straps, neckties, ropes, wires, ribbons, roads, snakes, fish*), one-sheet table **yì-djǎng djwǝ̄-dz** (sheet *for maps, boards, tables, bedsheets, rugs*) one-stem stick **yì-gǝ̄n gùn-dz** (stem *for poles, posts, branches, smoking pipes, cigars, cigarettes*), one-structure house **yì-swǒ fáng-dz** (structure *for all kinds of buildings*)

onions **yáng-tsüng** (overseas-scallion)

only **djìr** (*sounds like* paper): only he **djír-yǒu tā yí-gǝ rǝ́n** (only-have him one person), he ate only onions **tā djìr-chìr yáng-tsüng** (he only-eat onion)

open, not closed **kāi-dǝ** (open-belonging); open up **kāi** (*also* turn on, start): open the door **kāi-mǝ́n**

opinion, idea **yì-djyan** (mind-perceive)

opium **yǎ-pyàn** (*like English*)

opposite side **dwòi-myàn**; opposite, reverse **shyāng-fǎn-dǝ** (reciprocal-reverse-belonging)

or **hǝ́-shir** (or-be) *or* **hái-shir** (still-be, *used in questions asking a choice of possibilities*): I want him or you **wǒ yàu tā hǝ́-shir nǐ**, is it one or two? **shìr yí-gǝ hái-shir lyǎng-gǝ** (be one still-be two)

oranges **chǝ́n-dz**

orchestra **yuȝ-dwȝi** (music-team) *or* **gwǎn-shyán-yuȝ-dwȝi** (pipe-string-music-team)

order, to command **mǐng-ling**

order, to put in an order for **dìng**

ordinary, plain, common **pǔ-tūng** (common-circulate)

ore **kwǎng** (*also* mine)

organization, to organize **dzǔ-djir** (combine-weave)

original, originally **bȝn-lái** (root-come)

original copy **djȝng-djäng** (main-sheet)

other **byȝ-də**

otherwise **bù-rán**: come earlier, otherwise you can't eat **lái dzǎu-yi-dyar, bù-rán djyȝu bù-kȝ-yi chǐr** (come early-one-bit, otherwise not-possible eat)

ought to **yǐng-gäi**: I ought to go **wȝ yǐng-gäi-chyù**

ounce **yǐng-lyǎng** (English-tael)

our, ours **wȝ-mən-də** (us-belonging)

out, move out **chū**; outside **wǎi-təu** (outer-end): go out **chū-chyu** (exit-go), come out **chū-lai** (exit-come), outside the house **dzǎi-fáng-dz wǎi-təu** (located-house outside), outsider **wǎi-rən** (outside-person)

outline **dǎ-gäng** (big-maindivision)

over, to pass over **gwȝ** (*same as* to cross, pass): overdue **gwȝ-chǐ** (pass-date), overweight **gwȝ-djùng** (pass-heavy)

overcoat **dǎ-yi** (big-clothes)

owe **chyàn**: he owes me some rice **tā chyàn-wə mǐ** (he owe-me rice)

own, have **yȝu**

owner **djǔ-rən** (master-person)

oxygen **yǎng-chǐ** (nourish-gas)

P

pack, haversack **bȝi-bāu** (back-wrap); animal pack **twȝ-bāu** (pack-wrap); one pack, one package **yǐ-bāu** pack horse **twó-mǎ**; pack saddle **twó-ān**

pack up **bāu-chi-lai** (wrap-up-come)

Pacific Ocean **Tài-ping-yáng** (Too-level-ocean)

paddle, oar **djyǎng**; to paddle, row **hwǎ** (*sounds like* slide)

page **yè** (*same as* leaf): one page **yí-yè** (one-leaf), page-one **dì-yi-yè** (sequence-one-leaf)

pagoda **bǎu-tǎ**

pail, tub, barrel **tǔng** (*also* hollow cylinder)

pain **tóng** (*also* hurts)

painful **tóng-də** (pain-belonging)

paint (walls, surfaces) **chǐ**, paint (pictures) **hwà**

paints **yóu-chǐ** (oil-lacquer): wet paint **yóu-chǐ méi-gān** (oil-lacquer haven't-dry)

pair **shwǎng**: one pair **yì-shwǎng**

pajamas **shwèi-yi** (sleep-clothing)

pale **bái** (*also* white)

pan **píng-dǐ-gwō** (flat-bottom-pot)

pants **kù-dz**

paper **djǐr**

paper, newspaper **bàu**

papers, documents **wén-dyàn** (document-articles)

parachute **djyàng-lò-sǎn** (descend-fall-umbrella)

paratroops **sǎn-bing** (umbrella-soldier)

parents **fù-mǔ** (father-mother)

park **gūng-yuán** (public-garden)

park (vehicle) **tíng** (*same as* stop)

parking lot **tíng-chē-chǎng** (stop-vehicle-field)

part, section, department **bù-fən** (section-division)

party, political faction **dǎng**

party, social affair **hwèi** (*also* celebration, meeting)

pass (way thru mountains) **shān-lù** (mountain-road) *or* **gwān** (*used in place-names*)

pass, go past **gwò** (*same as* to cross): we came past his house **wǒ-mən dzǒu-gwǒ tā-də fáng-dz** (we go-cross him-belonging house); in the past **gwǒ-chyù** (past-go)

pass to, hand to **dǐ-gəi** (transmit-give): please pass the sugar **chǐng bǎ-táng dǐ-gəi-wə** (take-sugar transmit-give-me)

paste **djyǎng-dz**

path, road **lù**; path, trail **shyǎu-lù** (small-road)

pattern, model **yǎng-shir** (shape-form)

pay, salary **shin-shwǒi** (firewood-water); to pay **fù-chyán** (pay-money)

peace **hǒ-píng** (harmonious-even)

peaches **táur** *or* **táu-dz**

peak **shān-dǐng** (mountain-top)

peanuts **hwā-shēng** (flower-born)

pears **lí** *or* **lí-dz**

pedal **tà-bǎn** (step-board)

peel, shell, rind **pí** (*same as* skin)

pen **gāng-bǐ** (steel-brush); fountain pen **dzìr-lái-shwǒi-bǐ** (self-come-liquid-brush)

pencil **chyān-bǐ** (lead-brush)

peninsula **bàn-dǎu** (half-island)

penis **shēng-djír-chǐ** (reproduction-device, *medical language*) *or* **dji-ba** (*coarse language*)

people **rǒn** (*same as* person)

pepper (black) **hú-djyǎu** (foreign-peppers)

peppers (green) **là-djyǎu** (hot-peppers)

per cent **bǎi-fēn-dj** (hundred-division-derived): five per cent **bǎi-fēn-dj wǔ** (hundred-division-derived five)

perhaps, maybe **kǒ-yi** (*also* allowed); perhaps he'll come **tā kǒ-yi lái** (he maybe come)

periscope **chyán-wàng-djǐng** (dive-gaze-lens, *because first used in submarines*)

permit **ràng**; a permit **shyú-kǒ-djèng** (permission-certificate) person, people **rə́n**

personal, private **dzìr-yùng-də** (self-use-belonging); personal, individual **gə̀-rə́n-də** (individual-person-belonging)

personnel **rə́n-yuán** (person-personnel)

persuade **shwə̄-fú** (speak-obey)

philosophy **djə́-shyuə́** (wisdom-study *or* wisdom-science)

phone, telephone **dyàn-hwǎ** (electric-words); to phone **dǎ-dyàn-hwǎ** (hit-phone)

phonograph **lyə́u-shə̄ng-djī** (retain-voice-machine)

photo **shyàng-pyǎr** (image-card)

physical training **tǐ-yù** (body-culture)

pick up (small thing) **ná-chi-lai** (pickup-up-come); pick up, raise (large thing) **tái-chi-lai**; pick up (by handle) **tǐ-chi-lai**; pick up, gather, receive **shə̄u-chi-lai**

pickax, mattock **shír-dzìr-gǎu** (cross-pick)

picture, photo **shyàng-pyǎr** (image-card)

picture, sketch **tú-hwǎ** (picture-drawing)

piece, lump **kwài**: a piece of cheese **yǐ-kwài chǐ-sir** (one-piece cheese)

pig, hog **djū**

pigeon **gə̄-dz**

pile, stack **dwə̄i**: a pile of sand **yǐ-dwə̄i shǎ-dz** (one-pile sand)

pills (round) **yàu-wán-dz** (medicine-sphere); flat pills, tablets **yàu-pyàn** (medicine-card)

pillow **djə̌n-təu** (pillow-head)

pilot of airplane **fə̄i-shíng-yuán** (fly-procede-personnel); boat pilot **dwə̀-shə̌u** (rudder-hand)

pin **djə̄n** (*also* needle); safety pin, brooch **byə́-djə̄n** (clasp-pin)

pinch **nyə̄**

pink **húng** (*same as* red) *or* **fə̌n-húng** (powder-red)

pipe, tube **gwǎn-dz**

pipe for smoking **yān-də̌u** (tobacco-dipper)

pistol **shǒu-chyǎng** (hand-smallarm)

pitcher **gwàn** (*also* can, tank)

pivot, axis, axle **djóu-dz**

place, space **dì-fang** (ground-locality)

plague **shǔ-yì** (rat-pestilence)

plain, ordinary, common **pǔ-tūng** (common-circulate)

plane, airplane **fēi-djī** (fly-machine)

plans **djì-hwa** (plan-sketch); to plan **dzwò djì-hwa** (make plans); to plan to **shyǎng** (*same as* think): he plans to go **tā shyǎng-chyù** (he think-go)

plant (growing thing) **djír-wu** (plant-thing); to plant **djùng** (*sounds like* heavy)

plant, factory **gūng-chǎng** (work-factory)

plate, dish **pán-dz**; plate (flat machine part) **bǎn-dz** (*same as* board)

platform, stage **djyǎng-tái** (speech-stage); loading platform **djwǎng-shyò-tái** (load-unload-stage)

play (in the theater) **shì**; to play **wán** *or* **wár**

please **chǐng** (*same as* request): please come **chǐng-lái** (request-come); to please **djyàu gāu-shìng** (make glad): I try to please him **wǒ yàu djyàu-ta gāu-shìng** (I want make-him glad)

plenty **gòu-lə**

pliers **chyán-dz**

plow **lí**; to plow **gēng-dì** (plow-soil)

plug, stopper **sāi-dz**

plus **djyā** (*same as* add): three plus one is four **sān djyā-yī shìr sìr** (three add-one be four)

plywood **sān-djyā-bǎn** (three-pressed-board)

pneumonia **fēi-yán** (lung-inflammation)

pocket **dōur** (*in Peiping area*) *or* **dài** (*same as* bag)

point, dot **dyǎn-dz**: geographical point **dì-dyǎn** (ground-point)

point, tapered end **djyǎr** *or* **djyàn-dz**

point out **djǐr-chu-lai** (point-out-come)

poison **dú** (*sounds like* read)

poke **chǔ**

poker (game) **pǔ-kè**

pole **gǎn-dz**: telephone pole **dyàn-shyàn-gǎn** (electric-wire-pole)

pole for carrying **byǎn-dan** (flattened-yoke)

police, policeman **djǐng-chá** (lookout-inspect); military police **shyàn-bìng** (law-soldier)

police station **gūng-ān-djyú** (public-peace-bureau)

polish shoes **shwǎ-shyé** (brush-shoe); shoe polish **shyé-yéu** (shoe-oil)

polite **kè-chi**

pond, lake **hú** (*sounds like* small pot)

pontoon bridge **fú-chyáu** (float-bridge)

pool of water **shwěi-táng** (water-pool)

poor **chyúng**

population **rén-kǒu** (person-mouth): it has a population of about one thousand **yǒu chà-bu-dwé yì-chyǎn-kǒu** (have approximately one-thousand-mouth)

porcelain, chinaware **tsír-chǐ**

pork **djū-rèu** (pig-meat)

port **hái-kǒu** (sea-mouth)

porter **tyāu-fu** (shouldercarry-fellow)

position, location **dì-dyǎn** (ground-point); position, situation **dì-wəi** (ground-situation)

positive terminal **yáng-djí** (positive-extremity)

possible **kě-yi** (*also* maybe, allowed): I think it's possible **wé-shyǎng kě-yi** (I-think possible)

post, pillar **djù-dz**

postage stamp **yéu-pyàu** (mail-ticket)

postoffice **yéu-djèng-djyú** (mail-bureau)

postponed, to postpone **yán-chï** (prolong-date): we'll postpone this **wǒ-mən yầu gǒi-djǝ-gǝ yǎn-chi** (we want give-
this prolong-date)

pot, jar **hú** (*sounds like* lake); Chinese shallow pot **gwǝ**;
deep pot **tǔng** (*same as* pail, barrel, tub)

potatoes **yáng-yǜ** (overseas-tuber) *or* **yáng-shān-yǜ** (over-
seas-mountain-tuber)

pottery, chinaware **tsïr-chï** (porcelain-ware); rough, un-
glazed pottery **táu-chï** (earthen-ware)

pound (of weight) **bằng**, *but the official weight unit is the*
kilogram **gūng-djin** (universal-catty)

pour **dầu** (*sounds like* reach)

powder **fǒn**: to powder (face) **chá-fǒn** (apply-powder)

powder, black powder **hǝi-yầu** (black-medicine); smokeless
powder **wú-yān hwǒ-yầu** (without-smoke fire-medicine)

power, strength **lï**: electric power **dyần-lï**, horsepower
mǎ-lï, one-horsepower **yǐ-pi mǎ-lï** (one-head horse-power),
man power **rǒn-lï** (person-power), water power **shwǒi-lï**

power plant **fā-dyần-chǎng** (issue-electric-factory)

practice **lyần-shi** (train-practice)

prepare, get ready **yǜ-bǝi-hǎu-lǝ** (previously-prepare-good-
done): we'll get ready right away **wǒ-mən djyầu yǜ-bǝi-
hǎu-lǝ** (we immediately prepare), get the house ready
bǎ-fáng-dz yǜ-bǝi-hǎu-lǝ (take-house prepare)

present, gift **lǐ-wu** (polite-thing)

president of a country **dà-dzúng-tǔng** (big-main-control) *or*
dzúng-tǔng; president of an organization **hwầi-djǎng**
(organization-senior); president of a school **shyầu-djǎng**
(school-senior)

press **yā**

pressure **yā-lï** (press-power)

pretend **djyǎ-djwǎng**: he pretends to be a good man **tā
djyǎ-djwǎng hǎu-rǒn** (he pretend good-person), he pretends to leave **tā djyǎ-djwǎng dzǒu** (he pretend walk)

pretty **hǎu-kàn** (good-look)

price **djyà-chyan** (cost-money)

priest, minister **djyàu-shir** (teaching-person)

principal, capital investment **bšn-chyan** (root-money)

principal, main **djǔ-yàu-də** (master-want-belonging) *or* **dà** (*same as* big)

principle **djǔ-yì** (master-principle)

printing, to print **yìn-shwǎ**: print shop **yìn-shwǎ-swš** (print-structure)

prison, jail **djyǎn-yù**

prisoner **fàn-rən** (violate-person); prisoner of war **fú-lwš** (*also* to capture)

private, personal **dzìr-yùng-də** (self-use-belonging) *or* **sìr**: private affairs **sìr-shìr**, personal letter **sìr-rš́n-də shìn** (private-person-belonging letter)

private (army) **š̀r-dšng-bing** (two-class-soldier)

probably **dwš̌-bàn** (more-half)

problem, question **wš̀n-tí** (ask-subject)

produce, give forth **chǔ** (*same as* out, exit)

profit **djwàn**

program, plan of activity **djì-hwà** (plan-sketch)

promise **yún-shyǔ** (fulfil-permit)

pronunciation, to pronounce **fā-yin** (issue-sound)

proof **fáng** (*same as* prevent): water proof **fáng-shwši** (prevent-water), waterproof clothes **fáng-shwši-yi**

prop up **djìr-chi-lai** (prop-up-come)

propaganda **shyuǎn-chwán**

propeller **twši-djìn-dji** (push-advance-machine)

prostitute **djì-nyǔ** (prostitute-female)

protect **bǎu-hu**

Protestant Christianity **Yš̌-sǔ-djyàu** (Jesus-teaching)

protractor **lyáng-djyǎu-chì** (measure-angle-device)

province **shšng** (*also* state)

public **gǔng-gùng**: public matter **gǔng-shìr**

pull **lắ**

pulley **hwá-chз̌** (slide-vehicle)

pump by pressure **dắ** (*same as* hit); pump by suction **chз̌u**
(*same as* suck): water pump **chз̌u-shwз̌i-djī** (suck-water-
machine) *or* **dá-shwз̌i-djī** (hit-water-machine)

punish **chз̌ng-fá**

pure **chún**

purple **dzǐr-də** (purple-belonging)

purpose **dzǔng-djǐr** (main-theme)

purse, wallet **chyán-bǎu** (money-wrap)

pus **núng** *or* **nз̌ng**

push **twз̌i**

put down, place **fàng** (*also* release)

put in order **djз̌ng-li**

put off, postpone **yán-chī** (prolong-date)

put on (shirt, pants, socks) **chwǎn**; put on (hat, gloves,
shoes, eyeglasses) **dài** (*sounds like* take along, lead)

put out, extinguish **shí**: put out fire **shí-hwз̌**, put out light
shí-dз̌ng

put together, combine **hз́-chi-lai** (together-up-come)

Q

quality **hǎu-hwài** (good-bad); good quality **hǎu** (*same as*
good)

quarrel **djз̌ng-chǎu**

quarry **kāi-shír-təu-də dǐ-fang** (open-stone-belonging place)

quarter, one fourth **sìr-fз̌n-dj yî** (four-division-derived one);
quarter of an hour **yí-kз̀-djǔng** (one-quarter-clock)

question, problem **wз̀n-tí** (ask-topic)

quick, fast **kwài**: we run fast **wз̌-mən-pǎu-də kwài** (we-run-
belonging fast)

quiet **ān-djing** (peace-silence)

quinine **kwз̌i-níng** (*like English*)

R

rabbit tù-dz (*means* homosexual *if applied to a person*)

rack, shelf djyǎ-dz (*also* frame)

radiator sǎn-rə̀-chǐ (disperse-heat-device)

radio wú-shyǎn-dyǎn (without-wire-electricity): radio station wú-shyǎn-dyǎn-tái (radio-stage)

radius bǎn-djìng (half-distance)

raft mù-pái (wood-arrangement)

rag pwə̀-bù (broken-cloth)

raid tə̄u-shí (steal-raid); air raid kŭng-shí

railroad tyə̌-lù (iron-road)

rain yǔ; it rains shyǎ-yǔ (down-rain)

raincoat yǔ-yî (rain-clothes)

rank (military) djyə̄-dji: what's your rank? nǐ shìr shə́mmə djyə̄-dji (you be what rank)

rat hǎu-dz (*same as* mouse) *or* dǎ-hǎu-dz (big-mouse)

raw shə̄ng-də (*same as* born-belonging)

razor gwǎ-lyǎn-dǎu (shave-face-knife)

reach, arrive dǎu (*sounds like* pour)

reach out shə̄n-chu-chyu (reach-out-go) *or* shə̄n-chu-lai (reach-out-come)

read dú (*sounds like* poison) *or* kǎn (*same as* look at)

ready hǎu-lə (good-done); get ready yù-bəi-hǎu-lə (previously-prepare-good-done)

really shír-dzǎi

rear hə̀u-təu (back-end): rear wheels hə̀u-lún (rear-wheel)

reason lǐ-yú

receipt shə̄u-tyǎu (collect-slip)

receive shə̄u-dǎu (collect-reach)

recognize rə̀n-də (acquaint-obtain)

record (phonograph) chǎng-pyǎn (sing-card); to make a recording gwǎn-yin (record-sound) records (written) **djì-lù**; to record (in writing) **shyǒ-shya-lai** (write-down-come)

recruit **djāu** (*also* beckon, hail)

rectum **gāng-mén** (anus-door, *medical word*) *or* **pǐ-gu-yǎn** (rump-eye, *plain language*)

red **húng**

Red Cross **Húng-shír-dzìr-hwòi** (red-cross-organization)

regiment **twán**

region **dì-fang** (*same as* place) *or* **bù-fən** (*same as* part)

register (at a hotel) **dēng-djì** (register-record)

register (mail) **gwà-hàu** (hang-number)

regulations **fǎ-gwēi** (method-rule)

reins **djyǎng-shəng** (bridle-rope)

relapsing fever **hwói-gwēi-rð** (return-back-hot)

relatives **chǐn-chi** (intimate-kinsman)

religion **dzūng-djyàu** (sect-teaching)

remember, keep in mind **djì-də**; remember, recall **shyáng-chi-lai** (think-up-come)

rental **dzǔ-chyán** (rent-money), to rent **dzǔ**: the rent is thirty dollars a month **dzǔ-chyan shìr sǎn-shir-kwài yí-gə yuð** (rent-money be thirty-piece one month), I want to rent a house **wǒ yàu-dzǔ yǐ-swǒ fáng-dz** (I want-rent one-structure house), he rents to us **tā dzǔ gói-wǒ-mən** (he rent give-us)

repair, rebuild **shyōu-li**; repair, sew up, patch up **bǔ-yi-bu** (mend-one-mend): repair the house **bǎ-fáng-dz shyōu-li-chi-lai** (take-house rebuild-up-come), repair the shoes **bǎ-pí-shyǒ bǔ-yi-bu** (take-leather-shoe mend-one-mend)

repair shop **shyōu-li-chǎng** (repair factory)

repellent **fáng-wén-yàu** (prevent-mosquito-medicine)

report, message **bàu-gàu** (report-tell)

reporter (newspaper) **djì-djǒ** (record-er)

representative, to represent **dài-byǎu**

republic **mín-gwó** (people-country)

request **chǐng** (*also* invite, please)

resemble **shyàng** (*sounds like* towards)

resistance, to resist **dǐ-kàng** (resist-withstand)

resistance (electrical) **dyàn-dzǔ** (electric-hinder)

rest up **shyǒu-shi**

restaurant **fàn-gwǎn** (food-establishment)

result, effect **djyǒ-gwó** (yield-fruit)

retreat **chè-twèi** (remove-withdraw)

return to, give back to **hwán-gəi** (repay-give)

return to a place **hwéi-chyu** (return-go) *or* **hwéi-lai** (return-come)

reverse, opposite **shyàng-fǎn-də** (reciprocal-reverse-belonging)

rib bone **lè-gǔ**; rib (in machine construction) **lè-tsái** (rib-timber)

rice (raw grain) **mǐ**; cooked rice **fàn** (*same as* food) *or* **mǐ-fàn** (rice-food); young rice plants **yāng**; mature rice **dàu-dz**; unhusked grain rice **gǔ-dz**

rich, wealthy **yǒu-chyán** (have-money)

ricksha **yáng-chē** (overseas-cart)

ride (animals) **chí** (*same as* straddle); ride (vehicles) **dzwò** (*same as* sit): ride a horse **chí-mǎ** (straddle-horse), ride a car **dzwò-chì-chē** (sit-gas-vehicle)

ridge **shān-djí** (mountain-spine)

rifle, small arm **chyāng**

right, correct **dwèi-lə**; one's rights **chyuán-lǐ**

right away **yí-kàn djyòu** (one-look then): I'll be right back **wǒ yí-kàn djyòu hwéi-lai** (I one-look then return-come)

right hand side **yòu-byan**: go right **shyàng-yòu-byan chyu** (towards-righthand-side go)

ring **chyuǎr** (*same as* loop)

riot **bàu-dùng** (burst-move)

ripe **shə́u** (*also* well-cooked, done)

rise up **chǐ-lai** (rise-come)

river, stream **hə́**: river bank **hə́-àn**

rivet **mǎu-dǐng** (hat-nail)

road **lù** (*also* path): main road, highway **dà-lù** (big-road), hard-surface road **yǐng-myàn-lù**

roast **shǎu** (*same as* burn) *or* **kǎu** (*same as* bake)

rock, stone **shír-təu** (stone-head)

rocket **hwə̌-djyàn** (fire-arrow)

rod **gǎn-dz** (*also* stick, shaft)

roof **fáng-dǐng** (house-top)

roll over, rotate **gǔn**

roll up **djyuǎn**; a roll of tape **yǐ-djyǎn dài-dz** (one-roll tape)

roller **gǔn-dz**; roller for flattening ground **nyǎn-dz**

room **wū-dz**; room, space **dǐ-fang** (*same as* place): there are three rooms in that house **nà-swə fáng-dz yə̌u sān-djyǎn wū-dz** (that-structure house have three-compartment room), there's no room **mə́i-yəu dǐ-fang** (haven't place)

root **gə̄n** (*sounds like* with)

rope, string **shə́ng-dz**

rotten, to rot **làn-lə**

rough (cloth, board, etc.), not smooth **tsū**; rough (terrain, road) **bù-píng** (not-level)

round, circular, ball-shaped **yuǎn**

round of ammunition **yǐ-fā dàn-yàu** (one-issue ammunition)

route **lù** (*same as* road)

row **pái**: a row of men **yǐ-pái rə́n** (one-row person)

row, paddle **hwá** (*sounds like* slide)

rub **tsā** (*also* scrape, scrub)

rubber **shyàng-pí** (elephant-skin)

rudder **dwə̌**

rug, carpet **dǐ-tǎn** (ground-blanket) *or* **shí-dz** (*same as* mat)

ruler, straightedge **chǐr** (*also* foot of measure)

rules, regulations **fǎ-gwài** (method-rule)

rumor **yáu-yan**

rump **tún-bù** (rump-section, *refined language*) *or* **pǐ-gu** (flatus-haunch, *plain language*)

run, flow **lyǒu**

run, go fast **pǎu**

run after, chase **djwài**

run away, escape **táu-dzǒu** (escape-leave)

running (machine) **kāi-dj-nə** (start-continue)

Russia **à-gwə**

ruts **chà-dzǒu-də yìn** *or* **yàr** (vehicle-go-belonging print)

S

sack, bag **dài**; a sackful **yí-dài** (one-sack)

sad **bài-āi-də**

saddle **ān-dz**

safe, out of danger **píng-ān** (level-peace) *or* **ān-chyuán**: he's safe **tā píng-ān**, that place is safe now **nà-li ān-chyuán-lə** (there safe-done), it's safe to go **kǒ-yi chyù-lə** (possible go-done)

sail **fán**; to sail (boats) **kāi** (*also* drive *and* open)

salt **yán**

salute, greeting, to salute **djìng-lǐ**

salvage **lǐ-yùng fài-wu** (benefit-use waste-things)

same, alike **yí-yàng** (one-manner) *or* **túng-yàng** (same-manner): this is the same as that **djà-gə gēn-nà-gə yí-yàng** (this with-that alike)

sample **yàng-dz** (*also* form)

sand **shā-dz**: sandbag **shā-dài**, sandpaper **shā-djǐr**, sand table **shā-pán** (sand-plate)

satisfied **mǎn-yì** (full-mind); to satisfy **ràng mǎn-yì** (allow full-mind): satisfy him **ràng-tā mǎn-yì** (allow-him full-mind)

Saturday **lǐ-bài-lyòu** (week-six)

save, keep bău-tsún (protect-keep)

save, avoid waste djyə́-shə̌ng (reduce-spare): save time shə̌ng shír-həu

save, rescue djyə̀u (*sounds like* then)

save face lyə́u-gə myə̀n-dz

saw (tool) djyù

say, speak shwə̄: he says we may come tā-shwə̄ wə̌-mən kə́-yi lái (he-speak we allowed come)

scale (for weighing) chə̀ng; measuring scale kə̄-dù (carve-degree); proportional scale bǐ-lǐ-chǐr (compare-example-ruler *or* ratio-ruler)

scalp tə́u-pí (head-skin)

school shyuə́-shyə̀u (study-school)

schoolmate túng-shyuə́-də (same-study-belonging)

scissors, shears djyə̌n-dz

scrape tsā (*also* scrub, rub)

scratch djwā (*also* grasp)

screen, curtain mù

screening wire tyə́-shā (iron-gauze)

screw lwə́-sir-dǐng (spiral-strand-nail)

screwdriver gə̌n-djwə̄i (drive-point)

sea hăi: seacoast hăi-ə̀n, seaport hái-kə̌u (sea-mouth)

seal tú-djang (chart-emblem)

searchlight tə̀n-djə̀u-də̄ng (seek-shine-lamp)

season djǐ: a season yí-djǐ (one-season), this season djə̀-yí-djǐ

second (of time) yǐ-myə̌u (one-second)

second one dǐ-ə̀r-gə (sequence-two-item)

secret mǐ-mi

secretary, clerk shū-dji (write-record)

section, department, part bù-fən (section-division)

sector dǐ-chyü (ground-area)

sedative djə̀n-dǐng-yə̀u (calm-medicine)

see **kàn-djyan** (look-perceive)

seed **djŭng-dz**

seem **hăū-shyang** (good-resemble): this seems good **djə̀-gə hăū-shyang shìr hăū-də** (this seem be good-belonging)

self **dzìr-djĭ**: do it yourself **nĭ dzìr-djĭ dzwə̀** (you self do)

sell **măi**

send (things) **sùng**; send (gifts to) **sùng-gəi** (send-give); send (people) **pài**

sentence, phrase **hwà** (*same as* words): one sentence **yí-djyù hwà** (one-phrase words)

sentry **wə̀i-bing** (guard-soldier)

separate, divide **fə̄n-kāi** (division-open)

sergeant **djŭng-shìr** (middle-noncom)

servant **yùng-rən** (use-person)

serve (food) **kāi-fàn** (open-food): dinner is served **fàn kāi-lə** (food open-done)

serve as **dzwə̀** (*same as* do): he served in the army **tā dzwə̀-bing** (he do-soldier)

set **tàu**: a set of books **yí-tàu shū** (one-set book)

set off **fàng** (*same as* let go)

set the table **băi djwə̄-dz**

seven **chī**

seventh **dì-chī-gə** (sequence-seven-item); one seventh **chī-fə̄n-dj yī** (seven-division-derived one)

seventy **chī-shir** (seven-ten)

sew **fə́ng**

sew up, patch up **bú-chi-lai** (patch-up-come)

sex intercourse **shìng-djyău**; to have sex relations **fā-shə̄ng gwăn-shi** (happen relations)

shadow **yĭng-dz**

shaft, rod, stock **găn-dz**: drive-shaft **djə̀u-găn** (axle-shaft)

shake, rock **yáu**

shake hands **lā-shə̆u** (pull-hand)

shallow **chyǎn** (*also* elementary)

shape, form **yàng-dz** (*also* sample, sort)

sharp-edged **djyǎn**; sharp-pointed **kwài** (*also* fast); six o'clock sharp **djǔn-lyàu-dyǎn** (exact-six-mark)

shave **gwā**: shave the face **gwā-lyǎn** (shave-face)

she, her **tā** (*same as* him, it)

sheep, goat **yáng** (*sounds like* ocean)

sheet (bed) **bài-dǎn** (cover-sheet)

sheet of paper **yì-djāng djǐr** (one-sheet paper)

sheet steel **gāng-pyàn** (steel-slice)

shelf, rack **djyà-dz** (*also* frame)

shell (artillery) **pàu-dàn** (cannon-shell)

shell, peel **pí** (*same as* skin) *or* **kàr**

shield **gāng-bǎn** (steel-board)

shift for gears **pái-dǎng** (arrange-thwart)

shine light on **djàu** (*also* to photograph)

shine shoes **shwā-shyá** (brush-shoes)

ship, boat **chwán**

shirt **chèn-yī** (lining-clothes)

shoes **shyá** (*in North China*) *or* **hái-dz** (*in South, sounds like* child); shoe-polish **shyá-yóu** (shoe-oil)

shoot, shoot at **shà**

shop, store **pù-dz**; to shop **mǎi-dūng-shi** (buy-things)

shop, workshop **djī-chì-fáng** (machine-house)

short (people) **ǎi**; short (things), low **dī**; short in length or time **dwǎn**: short circuit **dwǎn-lù** (short-road), short wave **dwǎn-bwà**

should, ought to **yīng-gāi**: I should go **wà yīng-gāi chyù**

shoulder **djyǎn-bǎng** (shoulder-wing)

shovel, spade **chǎn-dz**

show, point out **djǐr**: show it to me **djǐr gǎi-wə kàn** (point give-me look)

shrapnel **lyóu-sǎn-dàn** (pomegranate-sleet-shell)

shredded bit, strand **sīr** (*sounds like* silk)

shrine **myàu**

shut, close **gwǎn**

sick, sickness **bìng**; get sick **bìng-lə** (sick-done)

side, direction **byān**: one-side **yǐ-byān**, towards the north **shyàng-bǒi-byan** (towards-north-side), on this side of the hill **dzài-shān djə̀-byan** (located-hill this-side)

sight, aim **myáu-djǔn** (sight-accurate)

sign (advertising) **djāu-pai** (beckon-board); road sign **lù-pái** (road-board)

signal **shìn-hàu** (message-sign)

silk **sīr** (*also* strand, shred)

silly, foolish **shǎ**

silver **yín-dz**

sing **chàng-gə̄** (sing-song)

sink **chə́n-lə** (sink-done)

sisters **djyǒ-mə̀i**; older sister **djyǒ-djyə**; younger sister **mə̀i-məi**

sit **dzwə̀** (*sounds like* do, make); sit up **dzwə̀-chi-lai** (sit-up-come)

situation **chíng-kwàng** (fact-condition)

six **lyə̀u**

sixth **dì-lyə̀u-gə** (sequence-six-item); one sixth **lyə̀u-fə̄n-dj yì** (six-division-derived one)

sixty **lyə̀u-shir** (six-ten)

size **dà-shyǎu** (big-small); what size? **dwə̄-dà** (much-big)

sketch **yàu-tú** (essentials-picture)

skillful **shə́u-lyàn-də** (ripe-exercise-belonging)

skin, hide **pí**

skinny **shə̀u**

skirmish **chyán-shàu-djàn** (forward-sentry-fight)

skirt **chyún-dz**

sky **tyān** (*also* day)

sled, sleigh **shyuǒ-chǒ** (snow-vehicle)

sleeping **shwǒi-djyàu** (sleep-slumber); to fall asleep **shwǒi-djáu-lǝ** (sleep-attain-done)

slice **pyàn** (*also* thick sheet, card): a slice **yí-pyàn** (one-slice), three slices of meat **sān-pyàn-rǝu**, sliced meat **rǝu-pyàn** (meat-slice)

slip (woman's undergarment) **chǝn-chyún** underlayer-skirt)

slippery, to slide **hwá** (*sounds like* to paddle, row)

slope **shyǒ-myàn** (oblique-surface); degree of slope **shyǒ-dù** (oblique-degree)

slot **yǎn** (*sounds like* eye)

slow **màn**: go slow **màn-màn dzǒu** (slow-slow walk), the clock is slow **djǔng màn** (clock slow)

small **shyǎu**

smart, clever, intelligent **tsūng-ming** (clever-bright)

smell **wǒn**: it smells bad **bù-hǎu wǒn** (not-good smell), I smell it **wǒ wǒn-ta**, take a smell **wǒn-yi-wǝn** (smell-one-smell)

smile, grin **shyàu** (*also* laugh)

smoke **yǎn** (*also* tobacco); to smoke tobacco **chǒu-yǎn** (suck-tobacco) *or* **chǐr-yǎn** (eat-tobacco, *used in the south*)

smooth, flat, level **píng**

snake **shǒ**

sniper **dzǔ-dji-shǒu** (swoop-strike-hand)

snow **shyuǒ**; it snows **shyǎ-shyuǒ** (down-snow)

so, like this **djǒ-yàng** (this-manner): do like this **djǒ-yàng dzwǒ** (this-manner do), don't do this **byǒ djǒ-yàng**

soak **pàu** (*sounds like* cannon *and* bubble)

soap **yí-dz** (*North and Central China*) *or* **fǒi-dzǎu** (fat-pod)

socket for lamp **dǒng-tǒu** (lamp-head); tube socket **gwǎn-dzwǒ** (tube-seat)

socks, stockings **wǎ-dz**

soda water **chǐ-shwǒr** *or* **chǐ-shwǒi** (gas-water); baking soda

kǎu-myǎn-bāu-də sū-dǎ (bake-bread-belonging soda);
washing soda shǐ-yî-shang-də sū-dǎ (wash-clothes-belonging soda)

sofa shā-fā

soft rwǎn

soldering metal hàn-shí (solder-tin); to solder, weld hàn-chi-lai (solder-up-come)

soldier bing *or* djyün-rə́n (army-person)

solid, not hollow shír-shin-də (honest-heart-belonging); solid, not liquid gù-tǐ (firm-body)

solve, work out djyǒ-djyuə́

some, not all yǒu-də (have-belonging): some people do it yǒu-də rə́n dzwə̀, some things yǒu-də dǔng-shi, sometimes yǒu-də shír-həu

something dǔng-shi (*same as* thing): he wants something tā yàu dǔng-shi

someone yǒu-rə́n (have-person): someone was looking for you yǒu-rən djáu-nǐ (someone seek-you)

son ə́r-dz

song gə̄r

soon kwài (*same as* fast, *used with* lə): he'll arrive soon tā kwài lái-lə (he fast come-done)

sore, boil chwāng (*sounds like* window)

sore, painful tə́ng-də (pain-belonging)

sorry nán-shə̀u (hard-endure); sorry, regretful hə̀u-hwǒi; I'm sorry, excuse me dwə̀i-bu-chi (face-not-up)

soul, spirit lǐng-hún

sound, not defective djyàn-chyuán (healthy-whole)

sounds, noise shə̄ng-yin

soup tāng

sour swān (*also* acid)

south nán: in the south dzài-nán-byan (located-south-side), go south shyàng-nán-byan dzǒu (towards-south-side-walk

Soviet Union Sū-lyán

space, place **dǐ-fang** (ground-direction)

Spain **Shì-bǎn-yá**

spare tire **bèi-tǎi** (prepare-tire)

spark plugs **hwǒ-hwā-tóu** (fire-flower-head)

speak, say **shwǒ**: I speak with him **wǒ gēn-ta shwǒ-hwà** (I with-him speak-words)

speech, to make a speech **yǎn-shwǒ** (perform-speak)

spend money **fèi-chyán**

spike, nail **dìng-dz**

spirit, soul **líng-hún**; spirit, ghost **gwǒi**

spirit, enthusiasm **djìng-shən** (energy-expression)

spirits **djyǒu** (*same as* wine, liquor) *or* **shāu-djyǒu** (burn-wine)

spit, to spit **tǔ-tán**

splice, knot **djyē-tóu** (connect-head)

splint for fracture **djyā-bǎn** (compress-board)

splinter, chip **mù-pì-dz** (wood-fragment); splinter (in skin) **tsǐr** (*sounds like* stab)

split, to split **pì**; split, cracked along the grain **pì-lə** (split-done)

spoil, destroy **pwò-hwài** (break-bad)

spoiled, out of order **hwài-lə** (bad-done)

sponge **hǎi-myán** (sea-cotton)

spoon **sháu-dz**

sprain **nyǒu-shāng** (twist-injury)

spread something out **sàn**; spread out, deploy, disperse **sàn-kāi** (spread-open)

spring (metal) **tán-hwáng** (bounce-spring)

spring of the year **chūn-tyan**

spy, secret agent **djyàn-dyǒ** (meddle-report) *or* **djyān-shi** (traitor-mean); to spy **dǎng-djyàn-dyǒ** *or* **dǎng-djyān-shi**

squad (of soldiers) **bān**

square **fāng-də**

squeeze **djǐ**

stab **djǎ** *or* **tsǐr**

stable **mǎ-hàu** (horse-stable)

stack, pile **dwəi**: a stack of books **yǐ-dwəi-shū** (one-pile book)

staff (of assistants) **tsǎn-méu**

stage (in theater) **wǔ-tái** (act-stage)

stairs, stairway **léu-ti** (building-ladder)

stake, stump **djwǎng** (*sounds like* to load)

stamps **yéu-pyàu** (mail-ticket)

standing **djàn-dj** (stand-remain); to stand up **djàn-chi-lai** (stand-up-come)

star **shîng-shing**

start (machines) **kāi-kai** (open-open); start, begin **kāi-shǐr** (open-start): start the machine **bǎ-dji-chǐ kāi-kai** (take-machine start), start running **kāi-shír pǎu** (begin run)

state, province **shǒng**

station **djàn** (*also* stand): railroad station **hwǒ-chə̄-djàn** (fire-vehicle-station)

stationery **shìn-djǐr** (letter-paper)

stay, live in a place **djù**; stay, wait **dǒng**

steady, firm **wǒn**

steak **nyéu-pái** (cattle-slice)

steal **təu**

steam, vapor **djǒng-chǐ** (evaporate-gas)

steel **gāng**

steep **dǒu**

steering, to steer **djyà-shǐr**

step, pace **bù**: a step **yí-bù** (one-pace)

stick, rod, shaft **gǎn-dz**

stick on, attach with glue **djàn**

still **hái**: he's still walking **tā hái-dzǒu-dj-nə** (he still-walk-continue), he's still here **tā hái dzài-djə̀-li** (he still located-here)

stimulant **shîng-fə̀n-yàu** (feeling-stimulate-medicine)

stockings, socks **wà-dz**

stomach **wèi**

stone, rock **shír-təu** (stone-head)

stop movement **tíng-lə**; stop doing **byə́** (*same as* don't); stop, block, head off **lán-dju** (block-reside): the machine stopped **djî-chǐ tíng-lə**, he stopped the machine **tā bǎ-djî-chǐ tíng-lə** (he take-machine stop), stop that man **lán-dju nà-gə rə́n**, stop it **byə́ dzwò nà-yang** (don't do that-manner) *or* **byə́ nà-yang** (don't that-manner)

stopper, plug **sāi-dz**

store **pù-dz**; bookstore **shū-pù**; clothing store **yī-dyàn** (clothes-shop); drugstore **yàu-dyàn** (medicine-shop); grocery store **dzá-hwə-pù** (mixed-goods-store)

story, tale **gù-shir** (former-affair)

straddling **chí** (*also* to ride astride)

straight **yì-djír** (one-straight); straight line **djír-shyàn**

strap, band, tape **dài-dz** (*sounds like* bag)

strategy **djàn-lyuə̀** (fight-essentials)

stream, river **hə́**

street **djyə̄** (*sounds like* get, receive)

streetcar **dyàn-chə̄** (electric-vehicle)

strike, hit **dǎ**

strike, walkout **bà-gūng** (quit-work)

string, rope **shə́ng-dz**

strong physically **chyáng-djwàng** (strong-robust); strongly built **djyǎn-gu** (firm-solid)

strong point **djyù-dyǎn** (holding-point)

stuck on, glued **djān-dj** (stick-remain)

study, learn **shyuə́**; student **shyuə́-shəng** (study-person)

stuff, things **dūng-shi**

submarine **chyán-shwə́i-tǐng** (submerge-water-barge)

substitute material **dài-yùng-pǐn** (substitute-use-article)

substitute worker **tì-shəu** (substitute-hand); to substitute for **tì** subtract **djyǎn** (*also* minus)

success **chéng-gūng** (succeed-work)

suddenly **hū-rán**

suffer, hardship **shòu-kǔ** (endure-bitterness); suffer pain or sorrow **nán-gwò** (difficult-pass)

sugar, candy **táng** (*sounds like* swamp)

suggest **chū-djú-yi** (produce-suggestion)

suggestion **djú-yi**

suit **tàu** (*same as* set): a suit of clothes **yí-tàu yī-shang** (one-set clothing)

suitcase, trunk **shyāng-dz** (*also* large box)

summer **shyà-tyan** (*sounds like* down-day)

sun **tài-yang**

Sunday **lǐ-bài-tyān** (week-day)

supper, evening meal **wǎn-fàn** (late-meal); late supper **shyāu-yè** (nocturnal-night)

supplies **gùng-yìng-pǐn** (supply-reserve-article)

support, maintain **yǎng**; support, back **yǔng-hù** (surround-protect): his father supports him **tā-də fù-chin yǎng-dj-ta** (him-belonging-father maintain-continue-him), we support our leader **wǒ-mən yǔng-hù wǒ-mən-də lǐng-shyòu** (we back us-belonging leader)

sure **yí-dìng-dwèi** (definitely-correct): I'm sure of what I say **wǒ-shwǒ-də yí-dìng-dwèi** (I-speak-belonging definitely-correct)

surface **myàn**: top surface **shàng-myan**

surrender **tóu-shyáng**

surround **bāu-wéi** (wrap-encircle)

suspect **hwái-yí**

swamp **táng** (*sounds like* sugar)

sweat, perspiration **hàn**; to sweat **chū-hàn** (exit-sweat)

sweater **máu-yī** (wool-clothing)

sweep **sǎu**

sweet **tyán** (*sounds like* cultivated field)

sweet potatoes **shān-yù** (mountain-tuber)
swim **yóu-yŭng**
switch (electrical) **dyàn-mén** (electric-door)
switchboard **dzŭng-dji** (overall-machine)
swollen **djŭng**
sword **dà-dāu** (big-knife)

T

table **djwē-dz**
table, chart **byău** (*also* meter, watch)
tactics **djàn-shù** (fight-method)
tail **wǒi-ba** (*in the South*) *or* **yì-ba**
tailor **tsái-fəng** (cut-sew)
take, hold **bǎ**
take along, lead away **dài-chyu** (lead-go)
take away (small things) **ná-chyu** (pickup-go); take away
    (large things) **tái-chyu** (lift-go); take apart **chāi-shyò**
    (disassemble-unload)
take care of **djàu-ying** (lookover-respond)
take off (clothes) **twē** (*sounds like* to tow); aircraft takes off
    chǐ-fēi (up-fly)
take pictures **djàu-shyàng** (shine-image)
talk, speak **shwē** (*also* say)
tall, high **gāu**
tame **shyùn-lyáng-də** (tame-gentle-belonging)
tank (for storing liquid) **gwàn** (*same as* can); gas tank (on
    auto) **yóu-shyāng** (oil-box)
tank, armored fighting vehicle **tǎn-kə-chē** (tank-vehicle)
Taoism **Dàu-djyàu** (Way-teaching)
tape, band, strap **dài-dz** (*sounds like* bag); adhesive tape
    djyāu-bù (glue-cloth)
target **bǎ-dz**

tarpaulin **fán-bù** (sail-cloth)

taste, sample (food) **cháng** (*sounds like* long); tastes good **hǎu-chǐr** (good-eat); tastes bad **bù-hǎu-chǐr** (not-good-eat)

taxes **shwèi** (*sounds like* sleep)

tea **chá**: tea leaves **chá-yè**

teach **djyǎu** (*sounds like* glue)

teacher **shyān-shəng** (first-born, *same as* Mister *and* husband)

tear up **sǐr** (*also* shredded bit, *sounds like* silk); tear apart **sǐr-kai** (tear-open)

tears (from the eyes) **yǎn-lèi** (eye-tears)

telegram **dyàn-bàu** (electric-report): to telegraph **dǎ-dyàn-bàu** (hit-telegram), telegraph set **dyàn-bàu-dji** (telegram-machine), telegraph office **dyàn-bàu-djyú** (telegram-bureau)

telephone **dyàn-hwà** (electric-words): to telephone **dǎ-dyàn-hwà** (hit-phone), phone him **dǎ-dyàn-hwà gəi-ta** (hit-phone give-him)

telescope **wàng-yuǎn-djìng** (gaze-distance-lens)

tell about, inform **gàu-sung**; tell, request, order **djyàu** (*sounds like* called): tell him about that **gàu-sung-ta nà-gə** (inform-him that), tell him to come **djyàu-ta lái** (order-him come)

temperature **wēn-dù** (warm-degree)

ten **shír**

tenth **dì-shír-gə** (sequence-ten-item); one tenth **shír-fən-dj yǐ** (ten-division-derived one)

tent **djàng-póng** (canopy-tent)

temple **myàu**

terraced fields **ti-tyán** (ladder-field)

terrain **dì-shíng** (earth-shape)

tetanus, lockjaw **pwè-shāng-fēng** (break-injury-wind)

146   *A PRACTICAL*

Thailand **Tài-gwə**; Thailander **Tài-gwə-rən** (Thai-country-
person)

than **bǐ** (*same as* compare): I am bigger than he **wǒ bǐ-tā dà**
(I compare-him big)

thanks **shyè-shyə**; many thanks **dwō-shyè**

that **nà-gə** *or* **nèi-gə**; that side **nà-byan**; in that way **nà-
yang** (that-manner)

thatch **tsǎu** (*same as* grass)

the **nà-gə** *or* **nèi-gə** (*same as* that, *but usually omitted*)

theater **dyàn-yǐng-yuàn** (movie-court) *or* **shì-yuàn-dz**
(drama-court)

their, theirs **tā-mən-də** (them-belonging)

them, they **tā-mən**

then, at that time **nà-gə shír-həu** (that-time); then, in that
case **djyòu** (*also* right away)

there **nàr** (*around Peiping*) *or* **nà-li** (that-in): he's there **tā
dzài-nà-li** (he located-there), he went there **tā dàu-nà-li
chyu** (he reach-there go)

therefore **swó-yi**

thermometer **wēn-dù-byǎu** (warm-degree-gage)

thermos bottle **nwán-shwěi-hú** (warm-water-jar)

these **djè-shyə** (this-some)

they, them **tā-mən** (*used for people*) *or* **tā** (*same as* it, *used
for things*): we meet them **wǒ-mən pèng-djyan ta-mən**,
I eat them **wǒ chīr-ta**

thick **hòu** (*sounds like* behind)

thief **dzéi**

thigh **dà-twěi** (big-leg)

thin **báu** *or* **shì**

thing, object **dūng-shi**; thing, matter **shìr-ching** (matter-
condition)

think, believe **shyǎng**: think it over **shyǎng-yi-shyang**
(think-one-think), I think I'll come **wǒ-shyǎng wǒ lai**

(I-think I come), I believe it's so **wǒ-shyǎng shìr** (I-think be)

third one **dì-sān-gə** (sequence-three-item); one-third **sān-fən-dj yī** (three-division-derived one)

thirsty **yàu-hǒ** (want-drink) *or* **kǒ**

this **djə̀-gə** *or* **djə̀i-gə**; this side **djə̀-byan**; this year **djìn-nyan**; this week **djə̀-gə lǐ-bài**; this month **djə̀-gə yuə̀**; in this way **djə̀-yang** (this-sort)

those **nà-shyə** (that-some)

thousand **chyǎn**; ten thousand **wàn**: a thousand **yǐ-chyǎn** (one-thousand), nine thousand **djyǒu-chyǎn** (nine-thousand), thirty thousand **sān-wàn** (three-tenthousand)

thread **shyàn** (*also* wire); screw thread **lwǒ-shyàn** (spiral-thread)

three **sān**

throat **sǎng-dz**

throttle, accelerator **chì-mén** (gas-door)

thru **chwǎn-gwə** (thru-cross): go thru the tunnel **chwǎn-gwə dùng chyu** (thru tunnel go)

throw **rə̄ng**; throw away, discard **rə̄ng-kai** (throw-open): throw that away **bǎ-nà-gə rə̄ng-kai** (take-that throw-open)

thumb **dà-djǐr** (big-finger)

thunder **lə́i**; to thunder **dǎ-lə́i** (hit-thunder)

Thursday **lǐ-bài-sìr** (week-four)

Tibet **Shì-dzàng**: Tibetan **Shì-dzàng-də** (Tibet-belonging), Tibetan language **Shì-dzàng-hwà** (Tibet-words), Tibetan person **Shì-dzàng-rə́n** (Tibet person)

ticket **pyàu**

tide **cháu-shwǒi** (tide-water); high tide **gāu-cháu**; low tide **dī-cháu**

tie, cravat **lǐng-dài** (neck-band)

tie up **kún-chi-lai** (tie-up-come); tie a knot in **djǐ-chi-lai** (knot-up-come): tie him up **bǎ-ta kún-chi-lai** (take-him tie-up-come), he tied a knot in the rope **tā bǎ-shǎng-dz djǐ-chi-lai** (he take-rope knot-up-come)

tight closed **gwān-djǐn-lə**; pulled tight **lā-djǐn-lə**; wedged tight **shyə̄-djǐn-lə**

till, until **dàu** (*same as* reach): till now **dàu-shyàn-dzài** (reach-now)

time **shír-həu**: there's no time **méi-yəu shír-həu** (haven't time); one-time, once **yí-tsìr**

tin **shí-la**

tip (money for service) **shyǎu-fə̀i** (small-spend)

tire (auto) **chə̄-tāi** (vehicle-tire)

tired out **lə̀i**

to **dàu** (*same as* reach) *or* **gə̌i** (*same as* give) *or omit*: he goes to Shanghai **tā dàu-Shàng-hǎi chyu** (he reach-Shanghai go), sell it to him **mài gəi-ta** (sell give-him), he came to tell us **tā lái gàu-sung wə-mən** (he come inform us)

tobacco, cigarettes **yān** (*also* smoke)

today **djīn-tyan** (present-day)

together **yì-chǐ** (one-rise); all together, in total **yí-gùng**

toilet **tsə̀-swə̌** (latrine-structure)

tomatoes **shī-húng-shìr** (west-red-persimmon)

tomorrow **míng-tyan** (morrow-day); day after tomorrow **hə̀u-tyan** (behind-day)

tonight **djīn-tyan wǎn-shang** (today evening)

too **tài**: too big **tài-dà**

tools **gūng-djyù** (work-gadget)

tooth **yá**

top, top-side **shàng-byan**; hilltop, peak **shān-dǐng**; house top, roof **fáng-dǐng**

torn **sīr-lə** (tear-done)

total, all together **yí-gùng**

touch **mwə̄**: don't touch that thing **byə̌ mwə̄ nà-gə dūng-shi** tourniquet **djír-shyuǒ-dài** (stop-blood-strap)

tow, drag **twǝ**

towards, facing **shyàng** (*sounds like* resemble): towards the east **shyàng-dūng-byan**

towel **shǒu-djin** (hand-napkin)

town, city **chéng**

tracks, footprints **djyǎu-yǝr** *or* **djyǎu-yìn-dz** (foot-print); vehicle tracks, ruts **chǝ-dzǒu-dǝ yǝr** (vehicle-go-belonging print); railroad tracks **tyǒ-lù** (iron-road, *same as* railroad)

trace, follow up **djwǝi-shyún**

tracoma **shā-yǎn** (sand-eye)

trade, commerce **mǎi-mai** (buy-sell); to trade, exchange **hwàn**

trader, merchant **mǎi-mai-rǝn** (buy-sell-person) *or* **shāng-rǝn** (commerce-person)

trailer **twǝ-chǝ** (tow-vehicle)

train **hwǒ-chǝ** (fire-vehicle)

training **shyùn-lyan** (teach-practise)

translate **fān-yi**

translator **fān-yi-yuán** (translate-personnel)

transmission, gear shift **byàn-sù-chì** (change-speed-device)

trap **shyàn-djǐng** (depression-pitfall); to trap **dǎi**

travel **lyǚ-shíng**

tray **pǎn-dz** (*also* plate)

treat **dài** (*sounds like* to lead): he treats me very well **tā dài-wǒ hén-hǎu** (he treat-me very-good); to stand treat **dzwǝ-djǔ-rǝn** (do-host-person)

tree **shù**

trench, ditch **gǝu**

triangle **sān-djyǎu-shíng** (three-angle-shape)

trick **djì-tsǝ** (calculate-strategem); to trick **shàng-dàng** (up-pawnshop): he tricked them **tā gǒi-tā-mǝn shàng-dàng** (he give-them up-pawnshop) trigger **băn-djĭ** (pry-machine)

trolley car **dyàn-chə̄** (electric-vehicle)

troops **djyŭn-dwə̀i** (army-team)

trouble **má-fan**

trousers **kù-dz**

truck **kǎ-chə̄** (car-vehicle)

true **djə̄n-də**: is it true? **shìr-bu-shir djə̄n-də** (be-not-be true)

true north **djə̀ng-bə̆i** (upright-north)

trunk, suitcase **shyǎng-dz** (*also* large box)

trust, believe **shyǎng-shìn**

truth **djə̄n-hwà** (true-words)

try **shìr-shir**: try to walk **dzə̆u-yi-dzəu shìr-shir** (walk-one-walk try-try)

tube, pipe **gwǎn-dz**; inner tube **lĭ-tāi** (inside-tire)

Tuesday **lĭ-bài-ə̀r** (week-two)

turn, become **lə** (*tacked-on syllable*, done): it turned sour **swān-lə** (sour-done)

turn, revolve **djwǎn-dùng** (turn-move); turn over, turn around **djwǎn-gwə-lai** (turn-cross-come)

turn on, switch on **kāi** (*same as* open, start); turn off **gwān** (*same as* close)

turtle **wǎng-ba** (king-eight; *to call a man turtle is an insult implying that his wife is unfaithful*)

twenty **ə̀r-shir** (two-ten)

twins **shwǎng-shəng** (pair-born)

twist **nyə̆u**

two **ə̀r** *or* **lyǎng** (**lyǎng** is used with classifiers and measure-words, **ə̀r** is used in saying the number by itself and in building the higher numbers): two people **lyǎng-gə rə́n**, two kilometers **lyǎng-gūng-lĭ**, two hundred twenty two people **ə̀r-bǎi-ə̀r-shir-ə̀r-gə-rə́n**

typewrite **dǎ-dzìr** (hit-letters)

typewriter **dǎ-dzìr-djī** (typewrite-machine)
typhoid **shāng-hán** (injury-chill)
typhus **bān-djə̀n shāng-hán** (spot-measles typhoid)

U

ugly **nán-kàn** (difficult-look) *or* **bù-hǎu-kàn** (not-good-look)
umbrella **sǎn**
under **dǐ-shya** (bottom-down): it's under the table **dzài-djwə̄-dz dǐ-shya** (located-table under), it went under the table **dàu-djwə̄-dz dǐ-shya chyu** (reach-table under go)
underclothes **lǐ-yī** (inside-clothes)
understand **dǔng**: do you understand? **dǔng-bu-dung** (understand-not-understand)
uniform **djyūn-fú** (army-dress)
union of workers **gūng-hwə̀i** (work-organization)
unite **lyán-hə́** (join-together)
United Nations **lyán-hə́-gwə́**
United States of America **Mə̌i-gwə** (*from* America, *interpreted to mean* beautiful-country)
universe **tyān-shyà** (sky-under)
university, college **dà-shyuə́** (big-school)
unload cargo **shyə̀-hwə̀**, unload (gun) **twə̀i-dzìr-dàn** (withdraw-cartridge)
untie **djyə̌-kai** (solve-open)
until **dàu** (*same as* reach): until tomorrow **dàu míng-tyan**
unwrap **dǎ-bāu** (hit-wrap) *or* **dǎ-kai** (hit-open)
up **shàng** (*same as* on): the sun comes up **tài-yang shàng-lai-lə** (sun up-come), I go up the hill **wə̌ shàng-shān chyu** (I up-hill go)
up, awake, arise **chǐ-lai** (riseup-come)
upstairs **lə́u-shang** (building-up)
upstream **shyàng-shàng** (towards-up) *or* **shàng-shwə̌i** (upwater): we walked upstream **wə̌-mən shùn-dj hə́ shyàng-**

shàng dzŏu (we alongside river towards-up walk), the boat went up the river **chwán shàng-shwŏi dzŏu-lə** (boat up-water go-done)

upright, vertical **shù-dj-də**

urgent **djĭn-djí** (tight-haste)

urine, urinate **shyăudz-byàn** (little-convenience)

us, we **wŏ-mən**

use **yùng**

use up **yùng-wán-lə** (use-finish-done)

useful **yŏu-yùng** (have-use)

usually **pŭ-tŭng** (*also* ordinary)

V

vacationing, on vacation **fàng-djyà-lə** (put-vacation-done)

vacuum **djŏn-kŭng** (true-empty)

valley **shān-gŭ** (*sounds like* mountain-drum)

valve **hwŏ-mén** (live-door)

vase **píng-dz** (*also* bottle)

vegetables **sù-tsài** (vegetarian-fooddish)

vehicle **chŏ**

vertical **shù-dj-də**

very, fairly **hŏn**

veteran, experienced soldier **lău-bĭng** (old-soldier); veteran, discharged soldier **twòi-wŭ-də bĭng** (retire-rank-belonging soldier)

vibrate **djòn-dùng** (shake-move)

vice-president **fù-dzúng-tŭng**

victory **shòng-lĭ**

vise **lău-hŭ-chyán-dz** (tiger-pliers)

village, very small town **tsŭn-dz**

visit **bài-wang** *or* **kàn** (*same as* see)

volt **fú**: fifty volts **wŭ-shir-fú**

voltage **dyàn-yā** (electricity-press)

voltmeter **dyàn-yā-byǎu** (electricity-press-meter)

volume (book) **bǒn-dz**: three volumes **sān-bǒn**

volume, cubic size **tǐ-djī** (body-cumulation); volume, cubic content **rúng-lyàng** (contain-quantity)

vomit **tù**

vote **shyuán-djǔ**

W

wagon **chǒ** (*same as* vehicle)

wait, wait for **dǒng**: wait a while **dǒng-yi-dəng** (wait-one-wait)

waiter **hwǒ-djì** (*also* clerk)

wake up, awake **shǐng-lə** (wake-done); wake someone **djyàu-shǐng** (call-wake): please wake me at seven o'clock **chíng-nǐ chī-dyan-djung djyàu-shíng-wǒ** (request-you seven-mark-clock call-wake-me); wake up! **shǐng-yi-shing** (wake-one-wake)

walk **dzǒu** (*also* leave): take a walk **dzǒu-yi-dzəu** (walk-one-walk) *or* **sàn-bù** (strew-steps)

wall **chyáng**

want **yàu** (*also* will)

war **djàn-djēng** (fight-strife)

warm, hot **rǒ**; the weather is pleasantly warm **tyān-chi nwǎn-hwə**

warn **djǐng-gàu** (warn-inform)

wash **shǐ**

washbasin **shí-lyǎn-pǒn** (wash-face-basin)

washer, gasket **dyàn-chyuān** (pad-loop)

waste, to waste **làng-fòi** (extravagant-spend)

watch, clock **byǎu** (*also* chart, meter)

watch, look on at **kàn**; watch over **kān** (*notice different tone from* look); watchman, to guard **shǒu-wòi**; to watch, shadow, keep an eye on **lyǒu-shòn** (detain-nerve) water **shwŏi**

watermelon **shî-gwa** (west-melon)

watt **wǎ** (*like English*): twenty watts **ər-shir-wǎ**

waves **lǎng-təu**; radio waves **dyàn-bwə̄** (electric-oscillation)

wax **là**

way, method **fá-dz**: there is no way out **méi-yəu fá-dz** (haven't way)

way, road **lù**: which way do we go? **wŏ-mən dǎ-shə́m-mə-lù dzŏu** (we hit-what-road go)

we, us **wŏ-mən**

weak **rwə̀**

weapon **bîng-chi** (soldier-device)

wear, put on (shirt, pants, socks) **chwān**; wear, put on (hat, tie, gloves, eyeglasses) **dài** (*sounds like* take along, lead)

weather **tyān-chi** (sky-gas)

weave (basketry, etc.), braid **byān**; weave (cloth), knit **djîr**

wedge **shyǎu-mù-pyàr** (small-wood-slice) *or* **shyə̄-dz**

Wednesday **lĭ-bài-sān** (week-three)

week **lĭ-bài**

weight **djùng-lyǎng** (heavy-measure); to weigh, in weight **djùng** (*also* heavy); to weigh (a thing) **chə̄ng-chəng**: this weighs five kilograms **djə̀-gə yŏu wŭ-gūng-djin djùng** (this have five-kilogram heavy), weigh this **bǎ-djə̀-gə chə̄ng-chəng** (take-this weigh)

welcome! **hwān-yíng**; you're welcome (in response to thanks) **bú-kè-chi** (not-courteous) *or* **byə́-kè-chi** (don't-courteous)

weld **dà-hàn** (big-solder)

well for water **djǐng**

well in health **hǎu** (*same as* good)

west **shî**: in the west **dzài-shî-byan** (located-west-side), go west **shyàng-shî-byan chyu** (towards-west-side go)

wet, damp **shir** (*sounds like* army division)

wharf **mǎ-təu** (*sounds like* horse-head)

what? **shǒm-mə**: what's this? **djǒ shìr shǒm-mə** (this be what), what kind of house? **shǒm-mə-yàng-də fáng-dz** (what-manner-belonging house) *or* **shǒm-mə fáng-dz**, what do you want? **nǐ yàu shǒm-mə** (you want what), what time is it? **djí-dyǎn-djūng-lə** (howmany-mark-clock-done)

wheat **mài-dz**; wheat foods **myàn-shir** (flour-edible)

wheel **lún-dz** *or* **gǔ-lur**

when? **shǒm-mə shír-həu** (what time); when, while **də shír-həu** (belonging time): when you came he was not home **nǐ-lái-də shír-həu tā bú-dzài-djyǎ** (you-come-belonging time, he not-located-home)

where? **shǒm-mə-dì-fang** (what-place) *or* **ná-li** *or* **nǎr**: where is he? **tā dzài-shǒm-mə-dì-fang** (him located-what-place), where's he going **tā dàu-shǒm-mə-dì-fang chyu** (he reach-what-place go)

which one? **nǎ-yí-gə** (which-one-item) *or* **nǒi-gə**

whistle **shàu-dz**; to whistle **chwǒi-shàu** (blow-whistle)

white **bái** (*also* pale)

who? **shǒm-mə-rən** (what-person) *or* **shwǒi**

whole **chyuán-tǐ** (whole-body)

whose? **shǒm-mə-rən-də** (what-person-belonging)

why? **wèi-shǒm-mə** (because-what)

wide **kwǎn**

wife, married woman **tài-tai** (*also* Mrs.)

wild **yǒ** (*sounds like* also); wild animal **yǒ-shòu** (wild-creature)

will **yàu** (*same as* want) *or leave it out*: he will go tomorrow **tā míng-tyan dzǒu** (he tomorrow leave)

willing **yuàn-yi** (willing-mind)

win victory **dǎ-shèng** (hit-victory); win money **yíng-chyán**

wind, breeze **fēng**

wind around **ràu-wǎr** *or* **ràu-wǎn-dz** (wind-bend)

window **chwǎng-hu**

wine, liquor **dyjǒu** (*sounds like* nine *and* long time)

wing **chǐr-bǎng**

winter **dūng-tyan**

wipe **tsǎ**

wire, cable **shyàn** (*also* thread); barbed wire **yǒu-tsǐr tyǒ-sǐr** (have-thorn iron-strand)

wise **tsūng-ming** (wise-bright)

wish **yàu-shir dwǝ̄-hǎu** (if, how-good): I wish I could **wǒ yàu-shir néng dwǝ̄-hǎu** (I if able, how-good); wish, pray **djú**: I wish you a safe journey **djú-nǐ yí-lù píng-ǎn** (pray-you one-road safe)

with, along with **gēn** (*also* follow); with, by **yùng** (*same as* use) *or* **dzwǝ̀** (*same as* sit): I come with him **wǒ gēn-ta lái** (I with-him come), I do it with a knife **wǒ yùng-dāu-dz dzwǝ̀** (I use-knife do), I come with the train **wǒ dzwǝ̀-hwǒ-chǝ̄ lái** (I sit-train come)

without **bù-gēn** (not-with) *or* **bú-yùng** (not-use): I come without him **wǒ bù-gēn-ta lái** (I not-with-him come), I cooked without salt **wǒ bú-yùng-yán dzwǝ̀-fàn** (I not-use-salt make-food)

woman **nyǔ-rən**

wood **mù-təu** (wood-head)

woods **shù-lín-dz** (tree-forest)

wool **máu-rúng** (hair-fuzz)

wool cloth **ní** (*sounds like* mud)

words, speaking **hwà**; written words, characters, letters **dzìr**

work, labor **gūng-dzwǝ̀** (work-do); work, business, matter **shìr** (*sounds like* be); to work **dzwǝ̀-gūng** (do-work) *or* **dzwǝ̀-shìr** (do-job)

worker **gūng-rən** (work-person)

workshop **djī-chì-fáng** (machine-device-house)

world **shìr-djyǝ**

worm **chúng-dz**

worn out, broken down **hwài-lǝ** (*also* spoiled); worn out, tired **lài**

worry **fā-chǒu** (issue-melancholy)

worship, attend services **dzwǝ̀ lǐ-bài** (do worship)

worship, admire **chúng-bài**

worse **hwài-yi-dyar** (bad-one-bit)

worst **dzwài-hwài** (most-bad)

wound, injury **shǎng**; wounded **fù-shǎng** (bear-injury)

wrap up **bǎu-chi-lai** (wrap-up-come)

wrench **bǎn-shǒu** (pry-hand)

write **shyǒ**: I can write **wǒ hwài-shyǒ-dzìr** (I knowhow-write-characters), write a letter **shyǒ-shìn**

wrong **tswǝ̀-dǝ** (mistake-belonging) *or* **tswǝ̀-lǝ** (mistake-done)

YZ

yams (one variety) **shǎn-yàu** (mountain-medicine); yams, sweet potatoes **shǎn-yù** (mountain-tuber)

yard, court **yuǎn-dz**

yard of length **mǎ** (*sounds like* horse), *but the official measure is the meter* **gūng-chǐr** (universal-lengthmeasure)

year **nyán**: one-year **yǐ-nyán**, this year **djin-nyan** (present-year), last year **chyù-nyan** (go-year), next year **míng-nyan** (morrow-year)

year old **swài**: a year old **yí-swài** (one-ageyear)

yellow **hwáng**

yes: *use expressions like* it's so **shìr** *or* it's O.K. **hǎu**

yesterday **dzwǒ-tyan** (yester-day); day before yesterday **chyán-tyan** (previous-day)

yet **hái** (*same as* still): has he come yet? **tā hái lái-bu-lai** (he still come-not-come)

yoke (for hitching) *or* carrying-pole (carried by one man)
  dàn-dz
you (one person) **nǐ**; you people **nǐ-mən**
young, youthful **nyán-chǐng** (year-light) *or* **shàu**; young,
  not grown up **shyǎu** (*same as* small)
your, yours **nǐ-də** (you-belonging) *or* **nǐ-mən-də** (youpeople-
  belonging)

zero **líng**

A CATALOG OF SELECTED
DOVER BOOKS
IN ALL FIELDS OF INTEREST

A CATALOG OF SELECTED DOVER
BOOKS IN ALL FIELDS OF INTEREST

DRAWINGS OF REMBRANDT, edited by Seymour Slive. Updated Lippmann, Hofstede de Groot edition, with definitive scholarly apparatus. All portraits, biblical sketches, landscapes, nudes. Oriental figures, classical studies, together with selection of work by followers. 550 illustrations. Total of 630pp. 9⅛ × 12¼.
21485-0, 21486-9 Pa., Two-vol. set $25.00

GHOST AND HORROR STORIES OF AMBROSE BIERCE, Ambrose Bierce. 24 tales vividly imagined, strangely prophetic, and decades ahead of their time in technical skill: "The Damned Thing," "An Inhabitant of Carcosa," "The Eyes of the Panther," "Moxon's Master," and 20 more. 199pp. 5⅜ × 8½. 20767-6 Pa. $3.95

ETHICAL WRITINGS OF MAIMONIDES, Maimonides. Most significant ethical works of great medieval sage, newly translated for utmost precision, readability. Laws Concerning Character Traits, Eight Chapters, more. 192pp. 5⅜ × 8½.
24522-5 Pa. $4.50

THE EXPLORATION OF THE COLORADO RIVER AND ITS CANYONS, J. W. Powell. Full text of Powell's 1,000-mile expedition down the fabled Colorado in 1869. Superb account of terrain, geology, vegetation, Indians, famine, mutiny, treacherous rapids, mighty canyons, during exploration of last unknown part of continental U.S. 400pp. 5⅜ × 8½. 20094-9 Pa. $6.95

HISTORY OF PHILOSOPHY, Julián Marías. Clearest one-volume history on the market. Every major philosopher and dozens of others, to Existentialism and later. 505pp. 5⅜ × 8½. 21739-6 Pa. $8.50

ALL ABOUT LIGHTNING, Martin A. Uman. Highly readable non-technical survey of nature and causes of lightning, thunderstorms, ball lightning, St. Elmo's Fire, much more. Illustrated. 192pp. 5⅜ × 8½. 25237-X Pa. $5.95

SAILING ALONE AROUND THE WORLD, Captain Joshua Slocum. First man to sail around the world, alone, in small boat. One of great feats of seamanship told in delightful manner. 67 illustrations. 294pp. 5⅜ × 8½. 20326-3 Pa. $4.50

LETTERS AND NOTES ON THE MANNERS, CUSTOMS AND CONDITIONS OF THE NORTH AMERICAN INDIANS, George Catlin. Classic account of life among Plains Indians: ceremonies, hunt, warfare, etc. 312 plates. 572pp. of text. 6⅛ × 9¼. 22118-0, 22119-9 Pa. Two-vol. set $15.90

ALASKA: The Harriman Expedition, 1899, John Burroughs, John Muir, et al. Informative, engrossing accounts of two-month, 9,000-mile expedition. Native peoples, wildlife, forests, geography, salmon industry, glaciers, more. Profusely illustrated. 240 black-and-white line drawings. 124 black-and-white photographs. 3 maps. Index. 576pp. 5⅜ × 8½. 25109-8 Pa. $11.95

THE BOOK OF BEASTS: Being a Translation from a Latin Bestiary of the Twelfth Century, T. H. White. Wonderful catalog real and fanciful beasts: manticore, griffin, phoenix, amphivius, jaculus, many more. White's witty erudite commentary on scientific, historical aspects. Fascinating glimpse of medieval mind. Illustrated. 296pp. 5⅜ × 8¼. (Available in U.S. only) 24609-4 Pa. $5.95

FRANK LLOYD WRIGHT: ARCHITECTURE AND NATURE With 160 Illustrations, Donald Hoffmann. Profusely illustrated study of influence of nature—especially prairie—on Wright's designs for Fallingwater, Robie House, Guggenheim Museum, other masterpieces. 96pp. 9¼ × 10¾. 25098-9 Pa. $7.95

FRANK LLOYD WRIGHT'S FALLINGWATER, Donald Hoffmann. Wright's famous waterfall house: planning and construction of organic idea. History of site, owners, Wright's personal involvement. Photographs of various stages of building. Preface by Edgar Kaufmann, Jr. 100 illustrations. 112pp. 9¼ × 10.
23671-4 Pa. $7.95

YEARS WITH FRANK LLOYD WRIGHT: Apprentice to Genius, Edgar Tafel. Insightful memoir by a former apprentice presents a revealing portrait of Wright the man, the inspired teacher, the greatest American architect. 372 black-and-white illustrations. Preface. Index. vi + 228pp. 8¼ × 11. 24801-1 Pa. $9.95

THE STORY OF KING ARTHUR AND HIS KNIGHTS, Howard Pyle. Enchanting version of King Arthur fable has delighted generations with imaginative narratives of exciting adventures and unforgettable illustrations by the author. 41 illustrations. xviii + 313pp. 6⅛ × 9¼. 21445-1 Pa. $5.95

THE GODS OF THE EGYPTIANS, E. A. Wallis Budge. Thorough coverage of numerous gods of ancient Egypt by foremost Egyptologist. Information on evolution of cults, rites and gods; the cult of Osiris; the Book of the Dead and its rites; the sacred animals and birds; Heaven and Hell; and more. 956pp. 6⅛ × 9¼.
22055-9, 22056-7 Pa., Two-vol. set $20.00

A THEOLOGICO-POLITICAL TREATISE, Benedict Spinoza. Also contains unfinished *Political Treatise*. Great classic on religious liberty, theory of government on common consent. R. Elwes translation. Total of 421pp. 5⅜ × 8½.
20249-6 Pa. $6.95

INCIDENTS OF TRAVEL IN CENTRAL AMERICA, CHIAPAS, AND YUCATAN, John L. Stephens. Almost single-handed discovery of Maya culture; exploration of ruined cities, monuments, temples; customs of Indians. 115 drawings. 892pp. 5⅜ × 8½. 22404-X, 22405-8 Pa., Two-vol. set $15.90

LOS CAPRICHOS, Francisco Goya. 80 plates of wild, grotesque monsters and caricatures. Prado manuscript included. 183pp. 6⅝ × 9⅝. 22384-1 Pa. $4.95

AUTOBIOGRAPHY: The Story of My Experiments with Truth, Mohandas K. Gandhi. Not hagiography, but Gandhi in his own words. Boyhood, legal studies, purification, the growth of the Satyagraha (nonviolent protest) movement. Critical, inspiring work of the man who freed India. 480pp. 5⅜ × 8½. (Available in U.S. only)
24593-4 Pa. $6.95

ILLUSTRATED DICTIONARY OF HISTORIC ARCHITECTURE, edited by Cyril M. Harris. Extraordinary compendium of clear, concise definitions for over 5,000 important architectural terms complemented by over 2,000 line drawings. Covers full spectrum of architecture from ancient ruins to 20th-century Modernism. Preface. 592pp. 7½ × 9⅝. 24444-X Pa. $14.95

THE NIGHT BEFORE CHRISTMAS, Clement Moore. Full text, and woodcuts from original 1848 book. Also critical, historical material. 19 illustrations. 40pp. 4⅝ × 6. 22797-9 Pa. $2.25

THE LESSON OF JAPANESE ARCHITECTURE: 165 Photographs, Jiro Harada. Memorable gallery of 165 photographs taken in the 1930's of exquisite Japanese homes of the well-to-do and historic buildings. 13 line diagrams. 192pp. 8⅜ × 11¼. 24778-3 Pa. $8.95

THE AUTOBIOGRAPHY OF CHARLES DARWIN AND SELECTED LETTERS, edited by Francis Darwin. The fascinating life of eccentric genius composed of an intimate memoir by Darwin (intended for his children); commentary by his son, Francis; hundreds of fragments from notebooks, journals, papers; and letters to and from Lyell, Hooker, Huxley, Wallace and Henslow. xi + 365pp. 5⅜ × 8. 20479-0 Pa. $5.95

WONDERS OF THE SKY: Observing Rainbows, Comets, Eclipses, the Stars and Other Phenomena, Fred Schaaf. Charming, easy-to-read poetic guide to all manner of celestial events visible to the naked eye. Mock suns, glories, Belt of Venus, more. Illustrated. 299pp. 5¼ × 8¼. 24402-4 Pa. $7.95

BURNHAM'S CELESTIAL HANDBOOK, Robert Burnham, Jr. Thorough guide to the stars beyond our solar system. Exhaustive treatment. Alphabetical by constellation: Andromeda to Cetus in Vol. 1; Chamaeleon to Orion in Vol. 2; and Pavo to Vulpecula in Vol. 3. Hundreds of illustrations. Index in Vol. 3. 2,000pp. 6⅛ × 9¼. 23567-X, 23568-8, 23673-0 Pa., Three-vol. set $36.85

STAR NAMES: Their Lore and Meaning, Richard Hinckley Allen. Fascinating history of names various cultures have given to constellations and literary and folkloristic uses that have been made of stars. Indexes to subjects. Arabic and Greek names. Biblical references. Bibliography. 563pp. 5⅜ × 8½. 21079-0 Pa. $7.95

THIRTY YEARS THAT SHOOK PHYSICS: The Story of Quantum Theory, George Gamow. Lucid, accessible introduction to influential theory of energy and matter. Careful explanations of Dirac's anti-particles, Bohr's model of the atom, much more. 12 plates. Numerous drawings. 240pp. 5⅜ × 8½. 24895-X Pa. $4.95

CHINESE DOMESTIC FURNITURE IN PHOTOGRAPHS AND MEASURED DRAWINGS, Gustav Ecke. A rare volume, now affordably priced for antique collectors, furniture buffs and art historians. Detailed review of styles ranging from early Shang to late Ming. Unabridged republication. 161 black-and-white drawings, photos. Total of 224pp. 8⅜ × 11¼. (Available in U.S. only) 25171-3 Pa. $12.95

VINCENT VAN GOGH: A Biography, Julius Meier-Graefe. Dynamic, penetrating study of artist's life, relationship with brother, Theo, painting techniques, travels, more. Readable, engrossing. 160pp. 5⅜ × 8½. (Available in U.S. only) 25253-1 Pa. $3.95

HOW TO WRITE, Gertrude Stein. Gertrude Stein claimed anyone could understand her unconventional writing—here are clues to help. Fascinating improvisations, language experiments, explanations illuminate Stein's craft and the art of writing. Total of 414pp. 4⅜ × 6⅜. 23144-5 Pa. $5.95

ADVENTURES AT SEA IN THE GREAT AGE OF SAIL: Five Firsthand Narratives, edited by Elliot Snow. Rare true accounts of exploration, whaling, shipwreck, fierce natives, trade, shipboard life, more. 33 illustrations. Introduction. 353pp. 5⅜ × 8½. 25177-2 Pa. $7.95

THE HERBAL OR GENERAL HISTORY OF PLANTS, John Gerard. Classic descriptions of about 2,850 plants—with over 2,700 illustrations—includes Latin and English names, physical descriptions, varieties, time and place of growth, more. 2,706 illustrations. xlv + 1,678pp. 8½ × 12¼. 23147-X Cloth. $75.00

DOROTHY AND THE WIZARD IN OZ, L. Frank Baum. Dorothy and the Wizard visit the center of the Earth, where people are vegetables, glass houses grow and Oz characters reappear. Classic sequel to *Wizard of Oz*. 256pp. 5⅜ × 8. 24714-7 Pa. $4.95

SONGS OF EXPERIENCE: Facsimile Reproduction with 26 Plates in Full Color, William Blake. This facsimile of Blake's original "Illuminated Book" reproduces 26 full-color plates from a rare 1826 edition. Includes "The Tyger," "London," "Holy Thursday," and other immortal poems. 26 color plates. Printed text of poems. 48pp. 5¼ × 7. 24636-1 Pa. $3.50

SONGS OF INNOCENCE, William Blake. The first and most popular of Blake's famous "Illuminated Books," in a facsimile edition reproducing all 31 brightly colored plates. Additional printed text of each poem. 64pp. 5¼ × 7. 22764-2 Pa. $3.50

PRECIOUS STONES, Max Bauer. Classic, thorough study of diamonds, rubies, emeralds, garnets, etc.: physical character, occurrence, properties, use, similar topics. 20 plates, 8 in color. 94 figures. 659pp. 6⅛ × 9¼. 21910-0, 21911-9 Pa., Two-vol. set $14.90

ENCYCLOPEDIA OF VICTORIAN NEEDLEWORK, S. F. A. Caulfeild and Blanche Saward. Full, precise descriptions of stitches, techniques for dozens of needlecrafts—most exhaustive reference of its kind. Over 800 figures. Total of 679pp. 8⅛ × 11. Two volumes. Vol. 1 22800-2 Pa. $10.95
Vol. 2 22801-0 Pa. $10.95

THE MARVELOUS LAND OF OZ, L. Frank Baum. Second Oz book, the Scarecrow and Tin Woodman are back with hero named Tip, Oz magic. 136 illustrations. 287pp. 5⅜ × 8½. 20692-0 Pa. $5.95

WILD FOWL DECOYS, Joel Barber. Basic book on the subject, by foremost authority and collector. Reveals history of decoy making and rigging, place in American culture, different kinds of decoys, how to make them, and how to use them. 140 plates. 156pp. 7⅞ × 10¾. 20011-6 Pa. $7.95

HISTORY OF LACE, Mrs. Bury Palliser. Definitive, profusely illustrated chronicle of lace from earliest times to late 19th century. Laces of Italy, Greece, England, France, Belgium, etc. Landmark of needlework scholarship. 266 illustrations. 672pp. 6⅛ × 9¼. 24742-2 Pa. $14.95

ILLUSTRATED GUIDE TO SHAKER FURNITURE, Robert Meader. All furniture and appurtenances, with much on unknown local styles. 235 photos. 146pp. 9 × 12. 22819-3 Pa. $7.95

WHALE SHIPS AND WHALING: A Pictorial Survey, George Francis Dow. Over 200 vintage engravings, drawings, photographs of barks, brigs, cutters, other vessels. Also harpoons, lances, whaling guns, many other artifacts. Comprehensive text by foremost authority. 207 black-and-white illustrations. 288pp. 6 × 9. 24808-9 Pa. $8.95

THE BERTRAMS, Anthony Trollope. Powerful portrayal of blind self-will and thwarted ambition includes one of Trollope's most heartrending love stories. 497pp. 5⅜ × 8½. 25119-5 Pa. $8.95

ADVENTURES WITH A HAND LENS, Richard Headstrom. Clearly written guide to observing and studying flowers and grasses, fish scales, moth and insect wings, egg cases, buds, feathers, seeds, leaf scars, moss, molds, ferns, common crystals, etc.—all with an ordinary, inexpensive magnifying glass. 209 exact line drawings aid in your discoveries. 220pp. 5⅜ × 8½. 23330-8 Pa. $3.95

RODIN ON ART AND ARTISTS, Auguste Rodin. Great sculptor's candid, wide-ranging comments on meaning of art; great artists; relation of sculpture to poetry, painting, music; philosophy of life, more. 76 superb black-and-white illustrations of Rodin's sculpture, drawings and prints. 119pp. 8⅜ × 11¼. 24487-3 Pa. $6.95

FIFTY CLASSIC FRENCH FILMS, 1912–1982: A Pictorial Record, Anthony Slide. Memorable stills from Grand Illusion, Beauty and the Beast, Hiroshima, Mon Amour, many more. Credits, plot synopses, reviews, etc. 160pp. 8¼ × 11. 25256-6 Pa. $11.95

THE PRINCIPLES OF PSYCHOLOGY, William James. Famous long course complete, unabridged. Stream of thought, time perception, memory, experimental methods; great work decades ahead of its time. 94 figures. 1,391pp. 5⅜ × 8½. 20381-6, 20382-4 Pa., Two-vol. set $19.90

BODIES IN A BOOKSHOP, R. T. Campbell. Challenging mystery of blackmail and murder with ingenious plot and superbly drawn characters. In the best tradition of British suspense fiction. 192pp. 5⅜ × 8½. 24720-1 Pa. $3.95

CALLAS: PORTRAIT OF A PRIMA DONNA, George Jellinek. Renowned commentator on the musical scene chronicles incredible career and life of the most controversial, fascinating, influential operatic personality of our time. 64 black-and-white photographs. 416pp. 5⅜ × 8¼. 25047-4 Pa. $7.95

GEOMETRY, RELATIVITY AND THE FOURTH DIMENSION, Rudolph Rucker. Exposition of fourth dimension, concepts of relativity as Flatland characters continue adventures. Popular, easily followed yet accurate, profound. 141 illustrations. 133pp. 5⅜ × 8½. 23400-2 Pa. $3.50

HOUSEHOLD STORIES BY THE BROTHERS GRIMM, with pictures by Walter Crane. 53 classic stories—Rumpelstiltskin, Rapunzel, Hansel and Gretel, the Fisherman and his Wife, Snow White, Tom Thumb, Sleeping Beauty, Cinderella, and so much more—lavishly illustrated with original 19th century drawings. 114 illustrations. x + 269pp. 5⅜ × 8½. 21080-4 Pa. $4.50

SUNDIALS, Albert Waugh. Far and away the best, most thorough coverage of ideas, mathematics concerned, types, construction, adjusting anywhere. Over 100 illustrations. 230pp. 5⅜ × 8½. 22947-5 Pa. $4.00

PICTURE HISTORY OF THE NORMANDIE: With 190 Illustrations, Frank O. Braynard. Full story of legendary French ocean liner: Art Deco interiors, design innovations, furnishings, celebrities, maiden voyage, tragic fire, much more. Extensive text. 144pp. 8⅞ × 11¾. 25257-4 Pa. $9.95

THE FIRST AMERICAN COOKBOOK: A Facsimile of "American Cookery," 1796, Amelia Simmons. Facsimile of the first American-written cookbook published in the United States contains authentic recipes for colonial favorites—pumpkin pudding, winter squash pudding, spruce beer, Indian slapjacks, and more. Introductory Essay and Glossary of colonial cooking terms. 80pp. 5⅜ × 8½. 24710-4 Pa. $3.50

101 PUZZLES IN THOUGHT AND LOGIC, C. R. Wylie, Jr. Solve murders and robberies, find out which fishermen are liars, how a blind man could possibly identify a color—purely by your own reasoning! 107pp. 5⅜ × 8½. 20367-0 Pa. $2.00

THE BOOK OF WORLD-FAMOUS MUSIC—CLASSICAL, POPULAR AND FOLK, James J. Fuld. Revised and enlarged republication of landmark work in musico-bibliography. Full information about nearly 1,000 songs and compositions including first lines of music and lyrics. New supplement. Index. 800pp. 5⅜ × 8¼. 24857-7 Pa. $14.95

ANTHROPOLOGY AND MODERN LIFE, Franz Boas. Great anthropologist's classic treatise on race and culture. Introduction by Ruth Bunzel. Only inexpensive paperback edition. 255pp. 5⅜ × 8½. 25245-0 Pa. $5.95

THE TALE OF PETER RABBIT, Beatrix Potter. The inimitable Peter's terrifying adventure in Mr. McGregor's garden, with all 27 wonderful, full-color Potter illustrations. 55pp. 4¼ × 5½. (Available in U.S. only) 22827-4 Pa. $1.75

THREE PROPHETIC SCIENCE FICTION NOVELS, H. G. Wells. *When the Sleeper Wakes, A Story of the Days to Come* and *The Time Machine* (full version). 335pp. 5⅜ × 8½. (Available in U.S. only) 20605-X Pa. $5.95

APICIUS COOKERY AND DINING IN IMPERIAL ROME, edited and translated by Joseph Dommers Vehling. Oldest known cookbook in existence offers readers a clear picture of what foods Romans ate, how they prepared them, etc. 49 illustrations. 301pp. 6⅛ × 9¼. 23563-7 Pa. $6.00

SHAKESPEARE LEXICON AND QUOTATION DICTIONARY, Alexander Schmidt. Full definitions, locations, shades of meaning of every word in plays and poems. More than 50,000 exact quotations. 1,485pp. 6½ × 9¼. 22726-X, 22727-8 Pa., Two-vol. set $27.90

THE WORLD'S GREAT SPEECHES, edited by Lewis Copeland and Lawrence W. Lamm. Vast collection of 278 speeches from Greeks to 1970. Powerful and effective models; unique look at history. 842pp. 5⅜ × 8½. 20468-5 Pa. $10.95

THE BLUE FAIRY BOOK, Andrew Lang. The first, most famous collection, with many familiar tales: Little Red Riding Hood, Aladdin and the Wonderful Lamp, Puss in Boots, Sleeping Beauty, Hansel and Gretel, Rumpelstiltskin; 37 in all. 138 illustrations. 390pp. 5⅜ × 8½. 21437-0 Pa. $5.95

THE STORY OF THE CHAMPIONS OF THE ROUND TABLE, Howard Pyle. Sir Launcelot, Sir Tristram and Sir Percival in spirited adventures of love and triumph retold in Pyle's inimitable style. 50 drawings, 31 full-page. xviii + 329pp. 6½ × 9¼. 21883-X Pa. $6.95

AUDUBON AND HIS JOURNALS, Maria Audubon. Unmatched two-volume portrait of the great artist, naturalist and author contains his journals, an excellent biography by his granddaughter, expert annotations by the noted ornithologist, Dr. Elliott Coues, and 37 superb illustrations. Total of 1,200pp. 5⅜ × 8.
Vol. I 25143-8 Pa. $8.95
Vol. II 25144-6 Pa. $8.95

GREAT DINOSAUR HUNTERS AND THEIR DISCOVERIES, Edwin H. Colbert. Fascinating, lavishly illustrated chronicle of dinosaur research, 1820's to 1960. Achievements of Cope, Marsh, Brown, Buckland, Mantell, Huxley, many others. 384pp. 5¼ × 8¼. 24701-5 Pa. $6.95

THE TASTEMAKERS, Russell Lynes. Informal, illustrated social history of American taste 1850's-1950's. First popularized categories Highbrow, Lowbrow, Middlebrow. 129 illustrations. New (1979) afterword. 384pp. 6 × 9.
23993-4 Pa. $6.95

DOUBLE CROSS PURPOSES, Ronald A. Knox. A treasure hunt in the Scottish Highlands, an old map, unidentified corpse, surprise discoveries keep reader guessing in this cleverly intricate tale of financial skullduggery. 2 black-and-white maps. 320pp. 5⅜ × 8½. (Available in U.S. only) 25032-6 Pa. $5.95

AUTHENTIC VICTORIAN DECORATION AND ORNAMENTATION IN FULL COLOR: 46 Plates from "Studies in Design," Christopher Dresser. Superb full-color lithographs reproduced from rare original portfolio of a major Victorian designer. 48pp. 9¼ × 12¼. 25083-0 Pa. $7.95

PRIMITIVE ART, Franz Boas. Remains the best text ever prepared on subject, thoroughly discussing Indian, African, Asian, Australian, and, especially, Northern American primitive art. Over 950 illustrations show ceramics, masks, totem poles, weapons, textiles, paintings, much more. 376pp. 5⅜ × 8. 20025-6 Pa. $6.95

SIDELIGHTS ON RELATIVITY, Albert Einstein. Unabridged republication of two lectures delivered by the great physicist in 1920-21. *Ether and Relativity* and *Geometry and Experience.* Elegant ideas in non-mathematical form, accessible to intelligent layman. vi + 56pp. 5⅜ × 8½. 24511-X Pa. $2.95

THE WIT AND HUMOR OF OSCAR WILDE, edited by Alvin Redman. More than 1,000 ripostes, paradoxes, wisecracks: Work is the curse of the drinking classes, I can resist everything except temptation, etc. 258pp. 5⅜ × 8½. 20602-5 Pa. $3.95

ADVENTURES WITH A MICROSCOPE, Richard Headstrom. 59 adventures with clothing fibers, protozoa, ferns and lichens, roots and leaves, much more. 142 illustrations. 232pp. 5⅜ × 8½. 23471-1 Pa. $3.95

PLANTS OF THE BIBLE, Harold N. Moldenke and Alma L. Moldenke. Standard reference to all 230 plants mentioned in Scriptures. Latin name, biblical reference, uses, modern identity, much more. Unsurpassed encyclopedic resource for scholars, botanists, nature lovers, students of Bible. Bibliography. Indexes. 123 black-and-white illustrations. 384pp. 6 × 9. 25069-5 Pa. $8.95

FAMOUS AMERICAN WOMEN: A Biographical Dictionary from Colonial Times to the Present, Robert McHenry, ed. From Pocahontas to Rosa Parks, 1,035 distinguished American women documented in separate biographical entries. Accurate, up-to-date data, numerous categories, spans 400 years. Indices. 493pp. 6½ × 9¼. 24523-3 Pa. $9.95

THE FABULOUS INTERIORS OF THE GREAT OCEAN LINERS IN HISTORIC PHOTOGRAPHS, William H. Miller, Jr. Some 200 superb photographs capture exquisite interiors of world's great "floating palaces"—1890's to 1980's: *Titanic, Ile de France, Queen Elizabeth, United States, Europa,* more. Approx. 200 black-and-white photographs. Captions. Text. Introduction. 160pp. 8⅞ × 11¾. 24756-2 Pa. $9.95

THE GREAT LUXURY LINERS, 1927–1954: A Photographic Record, William H. Miller, Jr. Nostalgic tribute to heyday of ocean liners. 186 photos of Ile de France, Normandie, Leviathan, Queen Elizabeth, United States, many others. Interior and exterior views. Introduction. Captions. 160pp. 9 × 12. 24056-8 Pa. $9.95

A NATURAL HISTORY OF THE DUCKS, John Charles Phillips. Great landmark of ornithology offers complete detailed coverage of nearly 200 species and subspecies of ducks: gadwall, sheldrake, merganser, pintail, many more. 74 full-color plates, 102 black-and-white. Bibliography. Total of 1,920pp. 8⅝ × 11¼. 25141-1, 25142-X Cloth. Two-vol. set $100.00

THE SEAWEED HANDBOOK: An Illustrated Guide to Seaweeds from North Carolina to Canada, Thomas F. Lee. Concise reference covers 78 species. Scientific and common names, habitat, distribution, more. Finding keys for easy identification. 224pp. 5⅜ × 8½. 25215-9 Pa. $5.95

THE TEN BOOKS OF ARCHITECTURE: The 1755 Leoni Edition, Leon Battista Alberti. Rare classic helped introduce the glories of ancient architecture to the Renaissance. 68 black-and-white plates. 336pp. 8⅜ × 11¼. 25239-6 Pa. $14.95

MISS MACKENZIE, Anthony Trollope. Minor masterpieces by Victorian master unmasks many truths about life in 19th-century England. First inexpensive edition in years. 392pp. 5⅜ × 8½. 25201-9 Pa. $7.95

THE RIME OF THE ANCIENT MARINER, Gustave Doré, Samuel Taylor Coleridge. Dramatic engravings considered by many to be his greatest work. The terrifying space of the open sea, the storms and whirlpools of an unknown ocean, the ice of Antarctica, more—all rendered in a powerful, chilling manner. Full text. 38 plates. 77pp. 9¼ × 12. 22305-1 Pa. $4.95

THE EXPEDITIONS OF ZEBULON MONTGOMERY PIKE, Zebulon Montgomery Pike. Fascinating first-hand accounts (1805–6) of exploration of Mississippi River, Indian wars, capture by Spanish dragoons, much more. 1,088pp. 5⅜ × 8½. 25254-X, 25255-8 Pa. Two-vol. set $23.90

A CONCISE HISTORY OF PHOTOGRAPHY: Third Revised Edition, Helmut Gernsheim. Best one-volume history—camera obscura, photochemistry, daguerreotypes, evolution of cameras, film, more. Also artistic aspects—landscape, portraits, fine art, etc. 281 black-and-white photographs. 26 in color. 176pp. 8⅜ × 11¼. 25128-4 Pa. $12.95

THE DORÉ BIBLE ILLUSTRATIONS, Gustave Doré. 241 detailed plates from the Bible: the Creation scenes, Adam and Eve, Flood, Babylon, battle sequences, life of Jesus, etc. Each plate is accompanied by the verses from the King James version of the Bible. 241pp. 9 × 12. 23004-X Pa. $8.95

HUGGER-MUGGER IN THE LOUVRE, Elliot Paul. Second Homer Evans mystery-comedy. Theft at the Louvre involves sleuth in hilarious, madcap caper. "A knockout."—Books. 336pp. 5⅜ × 8½. 25185-3 Pa. $5.95

FLATLAND, E. A. Abbott. Intriguing and enormously popular science-fiction classic explores the complexities of trying to survive as a two-dimensional being in a three-dimensional world. Amusingly illustrated by the author. 16 illustrations. 103pp. 5⅜ × 8½. 20001-9 Pa. $2.00

THE HISTORY OF THE LEWIS AND CLARK EXPEDITION, Meriwether Lewis and William Clark, edited by Elliott Coues. Classic edition of Lewis and Clark's day-by-day journals that later became the basis for U.S. claims to Oregon and the West. Accurate and invaluable geographical, botanical, biological, meteorological and anthropological material. Total of 1,508pp. 5⅜ × 8½.
21268-8, 21269-6, 21270-X Pa. Three-vol. set $25.50

LANGUAGE, TRUTH AND LOGIC, Alfred J. Ayer. Famous, clear introduction to Vienna, Cambridge schools of Logical Positivism. Role of philosophy, elimination of metaphysics, nature of analysis, etc. 160pp. 5⅜ × 8½. (Available in U.S. and Canada only) 20010-8 Pa. $2.95

MATHEMATICS FOR THE NONMATHEMATICIAN, Morris Kline. Detailed, college-level treatment of mathematics in cultural and historical context, with numerous exercises. For liberal arts students. Preface. Recommended Reading Lists. Tables. Index. Numerous black-and-white figures. xvi + 641pp. 5⅜ × 8½.
24823-2 Pa. $11.95

28 SCIENCE FICTION STORIES, H. G. Wells. Novels, *Star Begotten* and *Men Like Gods,* plus 26 short stories: "Empire of the Ants," "A Story of the Stone Age," "The Stolen Bacillus," "In the Abyss," etc. 915pp. 5⅜ × 8½. (Available in U.S. only) 20265-8 Cloth. $10.95

HANDBOOK OF PICTORIAL SYMBOLS, Rudolph Modley. 3,250 signs and symbols, many systems in full; official or heavy commercial use. Arranged by subject. Most in Pictorial Archive series. 143pp. 8⅜ × 11. 23357-X Pa. $5.95

INCIDENTS OF TRAVEL IN YUCATAN, John L. Stephens. Classic (1843) exploration of jungles of Yucatan, looking for evidences of Maya civilization. Travel adventures, Mexican and Indian culture, etc. Total of 669pp. 5⅜ × 8½.
20926-1, 20927-X Pa., Two-vol. set $9.90

DEGAS: An Intimate Portrait, Ambroise Vollard. Charming, anecdotal memoir by famous art dealer of one of the greatest 19th-century French painters. 14 black-and-white illustrations. Introduction by Harold L. Van Doren. 96pp. 5⅜ × 8½.
25131-4 Pa. $3.95

PERSONAL NARRATIVE OF A PILGRIMAGE TO ALMANDINAH AND MECCAH, Richard Burton. Great travel classic by remarkably colorful personality. Burton, disguised as a Moroccan, visited sacred shrines of Islam, narrowly escaping death. 47 illustrations. 959pp. 5⅜ × 8½.   21217-3, 21218-1 Pa., Two-vol. set $17.90

PHRASE AND WORD ORIGINS, A. H. Holt. Entertaining, reliable, modern study of more than 1,200 colorful words, phrases, origins and histories. Much unexpected information. 254pp. 5⅜ × 8½.   20758-7 Pa. $4.95

THE RED THUMB MARK, R. Austin Freeman. In this first Dr. Thorndyke case, the great scientific detective draws fascinating conclusions from the nature of a single fingerprint. Exciting story, authentic science. 320pp. 5⅜ × 8½. (Available in U.S. only)   25210-8 Pa. $5.95

AN EGYPTIAN HIEROGLYPHIC DICTIONARY, E. A. Wallis Budge. Monumental work containing about 25,000 words or terms that occur in texts ranging from 3000 B.C. to 600 A.D. Each entry consists of a transliteration of the word, the word in hieroglyphs, and the meaning in English. 1,314pp. 6⅜ × 10.
23615-3, 23616-1 Pa., Two-vol. set $27.90

THE COMPLEAT STRATEGYST: Being a Primer on the Theory of Games of Strategy, J. D. Williams. Highly entertaining classic describes, with many illustrated examples, how to select best strategies in conflict situations. Prefaces. Appendices. xvi + 268pp. 5⅜ × 8½.   25101-2 Pa. $5.95

THE ROAD TO OZ, L. Frank Baum. Dorothy meets the Shaggy Man, little Button-Bright and the Rainbow's beautiful daughter in this delightful trip to the magical Land of Oz. 272pp. 5⅜ × 8.   25208-6 Pa. $4.95

POINT AND LINE TO PLANE, Wassily Kandinsky. Seminal exposition of role of point, line, other elements in non-objective painting. Essential to understanding 20th-century art. 127 illustrations. 192pp. 6½ × 9¼.   23808-3 Pa. $4.50

LADY ANNA, Anthony Trollope. Moving chronicle of Countess Lovel's bitter struggle to win for herself and daughter Anna their rightful rank and fortune—perhaps at cost of sanity itself. 384pp. 5⅜ × 8½.   24669-8 Pa. $6.95

EGYPTIAN MAGIC, E. A. Wallis Budge. Sums up all that is known about magic in Ancient Egypt: the role of magic in controlling the gods, powerful amulets that warded off evil spirits, scarabs of immortality, use of wax images, formulas and spells, the secret name, much more. 253pp. 5⅜ × 8½.   22681-6 Pa. $4.00

THE DANCE OF SIVA, Ananda Coomaraswamy. Preeminent authority unfolds the vast metaphysic of India: the revelation of her art, conception of the universe, social organization, etc. 27 reproductions of art masterpieces. 192pp. 5⅜ × 8½.
24817-8 Pa. $5.95

CHRISTMAS CUSTOMS AND TRADITIONS, Clement A. Miles. Origin, evolution, significance of religious, secular practices. Caroling, gifts, yule logs, much more. Full, scholarly yet fascinating; non-sectarian. 400pp. 5⅜ × 8½.
23354-5 Pa. $6.50

THE HUMAN FIGURE IN MOTION, Eadweard Muybridge. More than 4,500 stopped-action photos, in action series, showing undraped men, women, children jumping, lying down, throwing, sitting, wrestling, carrying, etc. 390pp. 7⅞ × 10⅝.
20204-6 Cloth. $19.95

THE MAN WHO WAS THURSDAY, Gilbert Keith Chesterton. Witty, fast-paced novel about a club of anarchists in turn-of-the-century London. Brilliant social, religious, philosophical speculations. 128pp. 5⅜ × 8½.
25121-7 Pa. $3.95

A CEZANNE SKETCHBOOK: Figures, Portraits, Landscapes and Still Lifes, Paul Cezanne. Great artist experiments with tonal effects, light, mass, other qualities in over 100 drawings. A revealing view of developing master painter, precursor of Cubism. 102 black-and-white illustrations. 144pp. 8¾ × 6⅜.
24790-2 Pa. $5.95

AN ENCYCLOPEDIA OF BATTLES: Accounts of Over 1,560 Battles from 1479 B.C. to the Present, David Eggenberger. Presents essential details of every major battle in recorded history, from the first battle of Megiddo in 1479 B.C. to Grenada in 1984. List of Battle Maps. New Appendix covering the years 1967–1984. Index. 99 illustrations. 544pp. 6½ × 9¼.
24913-1 Pa. $14.95

AN ETYMOLOGICAL DICTIONARY OF MODERN ENGLISH, Ernest Weekley. Richest, fullest work, by foremost British lexicographer. Detailed word histories. Inexhaustible. Total of 856pp. 6½ × 9¼.
21873-2, 21874-0 Pa., Two-vol. set $17.00

WEBSTER'S AMERICAN MILITARY BIOGRAPHIES, edited by Robert McHenry. Over 1,000 figures who shaped 3 centuries of American military history. Detailed biographies of Nathan Hale, Douglas MacArthur, Mary Hallaren, others. Chronologies of engagements, more. Introduction. Addenda. 1,033 entries in alphabetical order. xi + 548pp. 6½ × 9¼. (Available in U.S. only)
24758-9 Pa. $11.95

LIFE IN ANCIENT EGYPT, Adolf Erman. Detailed older account, with much not in more recent books: domestic life, religion, magic, medicine, commerce, and whatever else needed for complete picture. Many illustrations. 597pp. 5⅜ × 8½.
22632-8 Pa. $8.50

HISTORIC COSTUME IN PICTURES, Braun & Schneider. Over 1,450 costumed figures shown, covering a wide variety of peoples: kings, emperors, nobles, priests, servants, soldiers, scholars, townsfolk, peasants, merchants, courtiers, cavaliers, and more. 256pp. 8⅜ × 11¼.
23150-X Pa. $7.95

THE NOTEBOOKS OF LEONARDO DA VINCI, edited by J. P. Richter. Extracts from manuscripts reveal great genius; on painting, sculpture, anatomy, sciences, geography, etc. Both Italian and English. 186 ms. pages reproduced, plus 500 additional drawings, including studies for *Last Supper, Sforza* monument, etc. 860pp. 7⅞ × 10¾. (Available in U.S. only) 22572-0, 22573-9 Pa., Two-vol. set $25.90

CATALOG OF DOVER BOOKS

THE ART NOUVEAU STYLE BOOK OF ALPHONSE MUCHA: All 72 Plates from "Documents Decoratifs" in Original Color, Alphonse Mucha. Rare copyright-free design portfolio by high priest of Art Nouveau. Jewelry, wallpaper, stained glass, furniture, figure studies, plant and animal motifs, etc. Only complete one-volume edition. 80pp. 9⅜ × 12¼. 24044-4 Pa. $8.95

ANIMALS: 1,419 COPYRIGHT-FREE ILLUSTRATIONS OF MAMMALS, BIRDS, FISH, INSECTS, ETC., edited by Jim Harter. Clear wood engravings present, in extremely lifelike poses, over 1,000 species of animals. One of the most extensive pictorial sourcebooks of its kind. Captions. Index. 284pp. 9 × 12.
23766-4 Pa. $9.95

OBELISTS FLY HIGH, C. Daly King. Masterpiece of American detective fiction, long out of print, involves murder on a 1935 transcontinental flight—"a very thrilling story"—NY Times. Unabridged and unaltered republication of the edition published by William Collins Sons & Co. Ltd., London, 1935. 288pp. 5⅜ × 8½. (Available in U.S. only) 25036-9 Pa. $4.95

VICTORIAN AND EDWARDIAN FASHION: A Photographic Survey, Alison Gernsheim. First fashion history completely illustrated by contemporary photographs. Full text plus 235 photos, 1840–1914, in which many celebrities appear. 240pp. 6½ × 9¼. 24205-6 Pa. $6.00

THE ART OF THE FRENCH ILLUSTRATED BOOK, 1700–1914, Gordon N. Ray. Over 630 superb book illustrations by Fragonard, Delacroix, Daumier, Doré, Grandville, Manet, Mucha, Steinlen, Toulouse-Lautrec and many others. Preface. Introduction. 633 halftones. Indices of artists, authors & titles, binders and provenances. Appendices. Bibliography. 608pp. 8⅜ × 11¼. 25086-5 Pa. $24.95

THE WONDERFUL WIZARD OF OZ, L. Frank Baum. Facsimile in full color of America's finest children's classic. 143 illustrations by W. W. Denslow. 267pp. 5⅜ × 8½. 20691-2 Pa. $5.95

FRONTIERS OF MODERN PHYSICS: New Perspectives on Cosmology, Relativity, Black Holes and Extraterrestrial Intelligence, Tony Rothman, et al. For the intelligent layman. Subjects include: cosmological models of the universe; black holes; the neutrino; the search for extraterrestrial intelligence. Introduction. 46 black-and-white illustrations. 192pp. 5⅜ × 8½. 24587-X Pa. $6.95

THE FRIENDLY STARS, Martha Evans Martin & Donald Howard Menzel. Classic text marshalls the stars together in an engaging, non-technical survey, presenting them as sources of beauty in night sky. 23 illustrations. Foreword. 2 star charts. Index. 147pp. 5⅜ × 8½. 21099-5 Pa. $3.50

FADS AND FALLACIES IN THE NAME OF SCIENCE, Martin Gardner. Fair, witty appraisal of cranks, quacks, and quackeries of science and pseudoscience: hollow earth, Velikovsky, orgone energy, Dianetics, flying saucers, Bridey Murphy, food and medical fads, etc. Revised, expanded In the Name of Science. "A very able and even-tempered presentation."—The New Yorker. 363pp. 5⅜ × 8. 20394-8 Pa. $5.95

ANCIENT EGYPT: ITS CULTURE AND HISTORY, J. E Manchip White. From pre-dynastics through Ptolemies: society, history, political structure, religion, daily life, literature, cultural heritage. 48 plates. 217pp. 5⅜ × 8½. 22548-8 Pa. $4.95

SIR HARRY HOTSPUR OF HUMBLETHWAITE, Anthony Trollope. Incisive, unconventional psychological study of a conflict between a wealthy baronet, his idealistic daughter, and their scapegrace cousin. The 1870 novel in its first inexpensive edition in years. 250pp. 5⅜ × 8½. 24953-0 Pa. $4.95

LASERS AND HOLOGRAPHY, Winston E. Kock. Sound introduction to burgeoning field, expanded (1981) for second edition. Wave patterns, coherence, lasers, diffraction, zone plates, properties of holograms, recent advances. 84 illustrations. 160pp. 5⅜ × 8¼. (Except in United Kingdom) 24041-X Pa. $3.50

INTRODUCTION TO ARTIFICIAL INTELLIGENCE: SECOND, EN-LARGED EDITION, Philip C. Jackson, Jr. Comprehensive survey of artificial intelligence—the study of how machines (computers) can be made to act intelligently. Includes introductory and advanced material. Extensive notes updating the main text. 132 black-and-white illustrations. 512pp. 5⅜ × 8½. 24864-X Pa. $8.95

HISTORY OF INDIAN AND INDONESIAN ART, Ananda K. Coomaraswamy. Over 400 illustrations illuminate classic study of Indian art from earliest Harappa finds to early 20th century. Provides philosophical, religious and social insights. 304pp. 6⅜ × 9⅜. 25005-9 Pa. $8.95

THE GOLEM, Gustav Meyrink. Most famous supernatural novel in modern European literature, set in Ghetto of Old Prague around 1890. Compelling story of mystical experiences, strange transformations, profound terror. 13 black-and-white illustrations. 224pp. 5⅜ × 8½. (Available in U.S. only) 25025-3 Pa. $5.95

ARMADALE, Wilkie Collins. Third great mystery novel by the author of *The Woman in White* and *The Moonstone*. Original magazine version with 40 illustrations. 597pp. 5⅜ × 8½. 23429-0 Pa. $7.95

PICTORIAL ENCYCLOPEDIA OF HISTORIC ARCHITECTURAL PLANS, DETAILS AND ELEMENTS: With 1,880 Line Drawings of Arches, Domes, Doorways, Facades, Gables, Windows, etc., John Theodore Haneman. Sourcebook of inspiration for architects, designers, others. Bibliography. Captions. 141pp. 9 × 12. 24605-1 Pa. $6.95

BENCHLEY LOST AND FOUND, Robert Benchley. Finest humor from early 30's, about pet peeves, child psychologists, post office and others. Mostly unavailable elsewhere. 73 illustrations by Peter Arno and others. 183pp. 5⅜ × 8½. 22410-4 Pa. $3.95

ERTÉ GRAPHICS, Erté. Collection of striking color graphics: *Seasons, Alphabet, Numerals, Aces* and *Precious Stones*. 50 plates, including 4 on covers. 48pp. 9⅜ × 12¼. 23580-7 Pa. $6.95

THE JOURNAL OF HENRY D. THOREAU, edited by Bradford Torrey, F. H. Allen. Complete reprinting of 14 volumes, 1837–61, over two million words; the sourcebooks for *Walden*, etc. Definitive. All original sketches, plus 75 photographs. 1,804pp. 8½ × 12¼. 20312-3, 20313-1 Cloth., Two-vol. set $80.00

CASTLES: THEIR CONSTRUCTION AND HISTORY, Sidney Toy. Traces castle development from ancient roots. Nearly 200 photographs and drawings illustrate moats, keeps, baileys, many other features. Caernarvon, Dover Castles, Hadrian's Wall, Tower of London, dozens more. 256pp. 5⅜ × 8¼. 24898-4 Pa. $5.95

AMERICAN CLIPPER SHIPS: 1833–1858, Octavius T. Howe & Frederick C. Matthews. Fully-illustrated, encyclopedic review of 352 clipper ships from the period of America's greatest maritime supremacy. Introduction. 109 halftones. 5 black-and-white line illustrations. Index. Total of 928pp. 5⅜ × 8½.
25115-2, 25116-0 Pa., Two-vol. set $17.90

TOWARDS A NEW ARCHITECTURE, Le Corbusier. Pioneering manifesto by great architect, near legendary founder of "International School." Technical and aesthetic theories, views on industry, economics, relation of form to function, "mass-production spirit," much more. Profusely illustrated. Unabridged translation of 13th French edition. Introduction by Frederick Etchells. 320pp. 6⅛ × 9¼.
(Available in U.S. only) 25023-7 Pa. $8.95

THE BOOK OF KELLS, edited by Blanche Cirker. Inexpensive collection of 32 full-color, full-page plates from the greatest illuminated manuscript of the Middle Ages, painstakingly reproduced from rare facsimile edition. Publisher's Note. Captions. 32pp. 9⅜ × 12¼. 24345-1 Pa. $4.50

BEST SCIENCE FICTION STORIES OF H. G. WELLS, H. G. Wells. Full novel *The Invisible Man,* plus 17 short stories: "The Crystal Egg," "Aepyornis Island," "The Strange Orchid," etc. 303pp. 5⅜ × 8½. (Available in U.S. only)
21531-8 Pa. $4.95

AMERICAN SAILING SHIPS: Their Plans and History, Charles G. Davis. Photos, construction details of schooners, frigates, clippers, other sailcraft of 18th to early 20th centuries—plus entertaining discourse on design, rigging, nautical lore, much more. 137 black-and-white illustrations. 240pp. 6⅛ × 9¼.
24658-2 Pa. $5.95

ENTERTAINING MATHEMATICAL PUZZLES, Martin Gardner. Selection of author's favorite conundrums involving arithmetic, money, speed, etc., with lively commentary. Complete solutions. 112pp. 5⅜ × 8½. 25211-6 Pa. $2.95
THE WILL TO BELIEVE, HUMAN IMMORTALITY, William James. Two books bound together. Effect of irrational on logical, and arguments for human immortality. 402pp. 5⅜ × 8½. 20291-7 Pa. $7.50

THE HAUNTED MONASTERY and THE CHINESE MAZE MURDERS, Robert Van Gulik. 2 full novels by Van Gulik continue adventures of Judge Dee and his companions. An evil Taoist monastery, seemingly supernatural events; overgrown topiary maze that hides strange crimes. Set in 7th-century China. 27 illustrations. 328pp. 5⅜ × 8½. 23502-5 Pa. $5.00

CELEBRATED CASES OF JUDGE DEE (DEE GOONG AN), translated by Robert Van Gulik. Authentic 18th-century Chinese detective novel; Dee and associates solve three interlocked cases. Led to Van Gulik's own stories with same characters. Extensive introduction. 9 illustrations. 237pp. 5⅜ × 8½.
23337-5 Pa. $4.95

Prices subject to change without notice.
Available at your book dealer or write for free catalog to Dept. GI, Dover Publications, Inc., 31 East 2nd St., Mineola, N.Y. 11501. Dover publishes more than 175 books each year on science, elementary and advanced mathematics, biology, music, art, literary history, social sciences and other areas.